MOTHERS, LOVERS, PRIESTS, PROPHETS, and KINGS

What the Old Testament Tells Us About God and Ourselves

MARY KATHARINE DEELEY

Liguori

LIGUORI, MISSOURI

Imprimi Potest: Thomas D. Picton, C.Ss.R.
Provincial, Denver Province, The Redemptorists

Published by Liguori Publications, Liguori, Missouri 63057
To order, call 800-325-9521 or visit www.liguori.org

Library of Congress Cataloging-in-Publication Data
Deeley, Mary Katharine
    Mothers, lovers, priests, prophets, and kings: what the old testament tells us about god and ourselves / Mary Katharine Deeley
    p. cm.
    ISBN 978-0-7648-1938-4
    L Bible. O.T.—Biography—Meditations. 2. Catholic Church—Prayers and devotions. I. Title. BS571.D38 2010
    242'.5--dc22

                                                         2010022269

Liguori Publications, a nonprofit corporation, is an apostolate of the Redemptorists. To learn more about the Redemptorists, visit Redemptorists.com.

Printed in the United States of America
14 13 12 11 10   5 4 3 2 1

CONTENTS

ACKNOWLEDGMENTS

So many people supported me during the writing of these reflections. My husband, Dan Lum, and my children, Kate and Annie, are a constant source of love and humor—they kept me going even when I thought I was out of ideas. A faithful band of readers set aside part of their busy lives to give me feedback on the sections. Rachel, Joe, Patrick, Dave, Cindy, Jen, Judy, Nikki, and Deb are just a few of the many students and associates who help make the Sheil Catholic Center what it is today. Thanks to each of you for making this book better. I particularly want to acknowledge Beth Deschryver, whose keen instincts helped me focus my message. The students, associates, and staff at Sheil provide opportunities for reflection through day-to-day encounters that enrich my ideas—thanks to all of you. The good people at Liguori Publications deserve my gratitude for inviting me to write for them, and Phoebe Collins deserves special thanks for her editing. Finally, I want to thank Father Ken Simpson, Father Dave Pavlik, and Father Paul Wachdorf—priests of the Archdiocese of Chicago—whose gentle guidance, prayer, friendship, and encouragement pointed to where God was in my life. They helped me hear what God was saying in Scripture, in prayer, and in my life. All three have been wonderful companions on the road, and I have been blessed by their presence.

INTRODUCTION

In the beginning of the school year, when we first start the process of the rite of Christian initiation of adults, I ask the participants and catechists to make a map of their lives in whatever way makes sense to them and to put on that map the important moments of their lives, however they define them. Inevitably, in the course of telling the stories attached to these moments, we come to know a good deal about each other and we reveal far more than we might in an ordinary "getting to know you" conversation.

Recently on the map I drew, I found myself putting down the moment I learned to read as a turning point. I remember sitting in the green chair in our living room with anything I could get my hands on (including, at one point, a cereal box) and reading out loud. When my mother asked what I was doing, I looked up at her and said very seriously, "I am reading with expression," a phrase I had, no doubt, heard in school.

It strikes me that reading with expression is a wonderful phrase for storytelling. "With expression" captures the wonder of reading that simultaneously manifests our emotions as we get caught up in the story and demonstrates the intent to squeeze out the characters and the situations so they inhabit our imaginations as living beings, teaching us about their world and ours and giving us another window through which we might see ourselves.

We can find the stories of our lives almost anywhere, even on a cereal box, but for Christians, one particular collection of stories helps to tell us who we are more than any other.

The Bible is our first library. In its pages we find people of virtue and vice, heroism and cowardice, holiness and sinfulness. The Bible tells about a God who is constant and surprising, judgmental and merciful. It is no secret that, for a Christian, the heart of the Bible resides in the gospels and the stories of Jesus of Nazareth in the New Testament.

One of my former students, a woman named Pattie, said that "the story of sacred Scripture turns on the life of one person, Jesus Christ." In the gospel narrative, we learn of God incarnate and walking among us as Jesus. Jesus heals the sick and raises the dead and, when the time comes, gives his life for those he loves. In fact, we might augment Pattie's comment by saying that the whole of Scripture turns on the life, death, and resurrection of Jesus of Nazareth.

In his story, we also learn our story: The God of Jesus is our God as well. We learn that God is in a relationship with us and that that relationship is familial—we are God's children.

John's first epistle adds that we do not know yet what we will become, but we do know that we are called to love one another and to love God, even if it means letting go of everything. We are invited, even challenged, to be disciples of Jesus, who is God with us. And we are part of a community of faith based on the apostles' witness and teaching.

It is also no secret that many Christians are far less familiar with the stories of the Old Testament (Hebrew Scriptures). Though we claim that the entire Bible reveals God to us and tells us the story of God's relationship with God's people, our knowledge of this other two-thirds of Scripture is limited to a few "fantastic tales," like the creation stories of Genesis, the Exodus narrative (thank you, Cecil B. DeMille and Steven Spielberg), and David and Goliath.

We might even reach into our memories for the story of Samson, whose haircut meant his capture but whose strength returned at the last second. And we might recall Ezekiel, who saw a wheel, or Elijah, who was caught up into heaven in a whirlwind.

Among the stories of women, we might have heard about Ruth and possibly about Sarah, but few others stand out. As a whole, though, Christians tend to neglect the Hebrew Scriptures for many different reasons. In classrooms and gathering spaces in the archdiocese of Chicago, people tell me they do not like "that Old Testament God," who has been portrayed to them as vindictive, judgmental, and arbitrary.

Still others find the language and the customs of the ancient Israelites confusing and inexplicable. A few more cite boredom as the reason for their neglect.

What few realize is that the God we meet in the Hebrew Scriptures is the God we meet in the Christian New Testament. The God of love and compassion and the God of war are the same God. Judgment and punishment occur in both the Old and the New Testaments, as do mercy and forgiveness.

In those moments when Christians do study the Hebrew Bible, it is hard to let go and let the text reveal its meaning and illuminate our understanding of God and ourselves. We tend to consider the Hebrew text important only if it speaks about Jesus, and so we read Jesus back into every text.

In truth, we cannot know God very well when we encounter him in the New Testament person of Jesus if we have not spent considerable time with God as we meet him in the Old Testament.

At the same time, the stories of Scripture, whether Old or New Testament, are stories about us as well. Every human strength and flaw has a place in these stories. Heroes, villains, people striving to lead faithful lives, and those simply caught up in the moment are on display as living word.

As they meet God and one another, so do we. Each of them adds a little more to the understanding of who we are and *whose we are* as we make our way in this world. Not only that, but the relationship between God and the world is told bit by bit in these stories.

Where else can we find mothers, lovers, judges, priests, and countless other characters who demonstrate so vividly the human struggle with faith and life? In subtle and not-so-subtle ways, they reveal, surprise, and engage us, moving us deeper and deeper into reflection on our life in God. Such stories are the expressions of our lives and of God's life with us, designed to convey in mere words what we have spent lifetimes trying to understand: that God loved the world.

The stories and meditations in this book are taken from the Hebrew Scriptures. Some will be familiar, some will be strange. All of them will bring us face to face with God in some way. In the course of storytelling, we will look at the backstory or context of the piece because context can illuminate and clarify an experience as well as give us a point of departure for our own stories.

We will also reflect on the stories themselves, stories of human experience that reveal so much about the One who made us, and which help us make sense of our experience with Jesus.

The oral tradition from which these stories come practically begs us to read them out loud first, and so I invite you to do that with as much expression as possible. Hearing the stories out loud often brings out words and meanings that remain hidden when we read silently, because our attention is focused on the text rather than on the appointment we have to keep later. We hear differently when we read out loud than when we read silently. We hear our words express what we feel about the story and, in that way, hear the stories as an expression of ourselves.

Following each story is a meditation for personal reflection and some questions for group sharing. All of them are designed to move us more deeply into our experiences with God. A final prayer invites the presence of God a little more intentionally and nudges us all a little closer to the divine.

MOTHERS

There are mothers who have given physical birth to their children and mothers (whether female or male) who have helped bring our souls and characters to birth by their compassion and attentiveness. Sometimes, these are the same people.

Many of us have been very fortunate to have more than one mothering influence in our lives, and they have taught us well about birth and death and everything in between. My mother taught me about making people welcome and about doing the best you can even if it does not happen to be what you want to do at the time.

Among the many people who "mothered" me in times of joy and grief and helped me grow are a Sister of Mercy and her wise counsel in hard times, a priest whose care for me in the period after the death of my parents was a gift from God, and my own sister whose humor left me breathless with laughter and restored my sense of perspective.

In these stories, we will meet four women—three mothers and a would-be mother—who greet the task of raising children who are not always their own with laughter, fear, courage, and forcefulness, and are shaped by that into women who come to know love in all its complexity.

They are a reminder to all of us that caring for another human being demands that we grow in our ability to love deeply, to let go, to ask for what we need, and to give whatever we can. We take our cue from God, who has done all of these things for us.

THE WOMAN WHO LAUGHED AT GOD

The LORD appeared to Abraham by the oaks of Mamre, as he sat at the entrance of his tent in the heat of the day. He looked up and saw three men standing near him. When he saw them, he ran from the tent entrance to meet them, and bowed down to the ground. He said, "My lord, if I find favor with you, do not pass by your servant. Let a little water be brought, and wash your feet, and rest yourselves under the tree. Let me bring a little bread, that you may refresh yourselves, and after that you may pass on—since you have come to your servant." So they said, "Do as you have said." And Abraham hastened into the tent to Sarah, and said, "Make ready quickly three measures of choice flour, knead it, and make cakes." Abraham ran to the herd, and took a calf, tender and good, and gave it to the servant, who hastened to prepare it. Then he took curds and milk and the calf that he had prepared, and set it before them; and he stood by them under the tree while they ate.

They said to him, "Where is your wife, Sarah?" And he said, "There, in the tent." Then one said, "I will surely return to you in due season, and your wife, Sarah, shall have a son." And Sarah was listening at the tent entrance behind him. Now Abraham and Sarah were old, advanced in age; it had ceased to be with Sarah after the manner of women. So Sarah laughed to herself, saying, "After I have grown old, and my husband is old, shall I have pleasure?" The LORD said to Abraham, "Why did Sarah laugh, and say, 'Shall I indeed bear a child, now that I am old?' Is anything too wonderful for the LORD? At the set time I will return to you, in due season, and Sarah shall have a son." But Sarah denied it, saying, "I did not laugh;" for she was afraid. He said, "Oh yes, you did laugh."

GENESIS 18:1–15

〰〰〰〰〰〰〰〰〰〰〰

The Backstory

We meet Sarah and Abraham in the book of Genesis, part of the Pentateuch or the first five books of the Bible. In these books, some of the great acts of God take place—Creation, the Flood, the Exodus, including the parting of the Red Sea. In fact, Jack Miles, in his biography of God, gives the Pentateuch the overarching theme of "God Acts." Included in those great acts is a promise given to a man and woman who had no reason to believe they were even noticed by God at all.

When we first meet Sarah (shortly before this story) we are gradually told three things about her: she is beautiful, she does not have children, and she isn't getting any younger.

For the ancient Israelites, children were the promise for the future. Not to have children was considered a tragedy.

Meanwhile, Sarah's husband, Abraham, had followed a God he didn't know from Ur to Canaan and had been given a promise of land, descendants, and blessing, not once, but twice. In an effort to please her husband and make God's promises come true, Sarah convinces him to have a child with her servant.

The second time Abraham hears the promise (Chapter 17), we are told that he is nearly a hundred, and Sarah is ninety years old. Abraham calculates the odds and figures that God must mean his son, Ishmael, borne of Hagar. It really didn't seem possible that Sarah and he could have a child.

At the same time, Sarah and Abraham live in the Middle East where the great tradition of hospitality requires that you greet strangers and make them welcome guests. Such strangers might simply be people looking for a place of shelter, or they might be angels bringing a blessing.

The practice is continued, not only in the Middle East, but in places like my mother's house where there was always enough for one more and always an extra gift at Christmas in case we met someone who needed a place to stay and a family with whom to celebrate.

In this story, Abraham does everything that is required, from greeting the strangers to running to the kitchen to instruct Sarah to running to the barn to instruct the servants in order to ensure that a wonderful feast is prepared for the strangers. Then he sits, expectantly it seems, for the word of thanks or blessing or honor that will surely come to him as head of the house. He leans forward eagerly as they open their mouths to speak.

And he is immediately surprised when the word that comes from the stranger's mouth is neither thanks nor a blessing, but a question: "Where is Sarah, your wife?" Sarah was where she always seemed to be, in the tent, at the table, and behind the scenes.

But the promise, the blessing, the gift of this stranger was hers: "I will return about this time next year and Sarah, your wife, will have a son." For the first time in this family drama, Abraham seems to realize that God's covenant and promise is not only about him. Up until this point, the promise of God came to him, and Sarah remained strangely silent through most of it. Now the focus is on Sarah, who remains listening carefully at the door of the tent.

While Abraham's reaction to the promise was surprise and a misunderstanding, Sarah bursts forth in recognition of the ludicrous. She laughs and draws the Lord's attention. She thinks about the impossibility of it all, knowing that time and age are often cruel with human bodies and human desires. And she and Abraham had not been able to have a child before this, no matter how hard they tried. Some things, she thought, are just not going to happen.

<hr>

What Does This Story Tell Us?

Sarah thought what God promised was impossible, but she is hardly the only person to have thought so. Her reasons are rational: She and Abraham are too old to have children, and nothing they had done to that point had helped.

Besides, she knew Abraham had been given this promise already and they had done their best to take care of it. What could the promise have to do with her now? We might all have a tendency to respond with very rational reasons when God calls to us or reveals a plan that seems impossible.

Some of us might even indulge in a little sarcasm: "Oh really?" But when we try to laugh God off and dismiss what we think God might be after, God's reaction is often uncomfortable in its simplicity. "Why did you laugh?" And we are caught. If we say we didn't laugh, God counters with, "Yes, you did," and waits patiently for the answer. God's response to Sarah makes us think a little bit.

The story of Sarah teaches us that God is undeterred by our disbelief or our sarcasm. Nor is God persuaded when we, for whatever reason, think that we cannot possibly be the person that God has in mind to get the job done.

For her whole life, Sarah thought that Abraham was the center of God's attention. So it seemed unusual that the stranger who had come to their door would ask about her and promise that she would have a son.

But she quickly found out that even those who live behind the scenes and out of the spotlight and who quietly go about their day-to-day lives can be the recipients of God's grace and attention just as much as those who live at the center.

God touches each one of us, whether or not we have done something that others would consider noteworthy.

What had Sarah done but stand with Abraham as he set off for unknown places and try to give him a son even if it could not be hers, and then prepare a feast for her husband to serve to strangers?

And confronted at last by God, listening to what he had in store for her, she did what many of us would have done. She laughed at the absolute surprise and absurdity of it all, especially when she realized what God wanted even after that. It was something that Jeremiah and Mary and Peter and countless others in the Old and New Testaments knew something about.

Neither Sarah nor we are the first people to think that what God wants is impossible. But impossible is, in some ways, what gets God up in the morning. What we often read in Scripture is God's eternal laughter and the question: "What impossible surprise can I spring on someone today?"

In story after story in the Old Testament, we read about God, who is unpredictable and unable to be captured in a single image. And finally, the Scriptures tell us about God's ultimate surprise: that somebody who died on a cross could be the savior of the world.

As a parenthetical note: In the Church's *Lectionary*, this story of Sarah and Abraham is paired with another story about God's bounty. Martha, having learned very well the lessons of her ancestor, Sarah, stood serving in the kitchen while her sister, Mary, sat listening at Jesus' feet. "Perhaps," Martha thought, "God's blessing will come to me in the kitchen as it did for Sarah. And if Mary wants a portion of the blessing, she should come and serve as I do."

Of course, Jesus surprises Martha as much as God surprised Abraham. Every one of us has a little of Abraham and Martha in us. And just when we think we have things figured out, along come Sarah and Mary to confound expectations and let us know that God's blessing and promise come to those whom God wills, wherever they may be.

‖‖‖‖‖‖‖‖‖‖‖‖‖‖‖‖‖‖‖‖‖‖

Meditation for Groups or Individuals

Sarah, like so many women and men both then and now, defines what's possible for herself by looking at age and her experiences (or lack of them) in her life. If we look at her whole story in Genesis, we will find that the narrator does the same and adds comments about her looks and whether she was a good wife to her husband.

We rarely hear her voice or her thoughts as she participates in the promise of God to give land, blessing, and descendants to Abraham. We do know that she felt keenly her inability to have children and desired to help her husband (and God) fulfill the covenant. She was, perhaps, resigned to the reality that she was not going to have a family of her own.

Did she reach a point where she simply decided to get on with her life whether she had children or not? Did she accept what seemed to be her destiny and stop worrying about it? We will never know that for sure, but her reaction to God's promise—made directly to her in her senior years—suggests as much.

So much of Sarah's story and reaction to God's promise touches us at our hearts. Female or male, we often define ourselves (or are defined by others) by pointing to what we can do or how old (or young) we are.

And sometimes we depend on the approval of others for our worth and rely on their perceptions to tell us who we are.

Then, just when we think we have figured it out, someone or something comes along that confounds our expectations and does the impossible.

Inevitably, that stranger is an instrument of God who shows us a capacity for life in us that we did not know existed.

Read the story of Sarah again and put yourself in her place. Think about or discuss the following questions:

In what ways do you feel you are like Sarah? In what ways are you different?

Has there ever been a time when you have decided that something was impossible for you, for whatever reason, and then been surprised that it happened?

Have there been moments in your life when someone, unexpected or unexpectedly, has shown you how much you are loved?
How would you describe the feelings around that moment?

Sometimes we are confronted with decisions to make about where we are going and with whom we are going to spend our time.

When we look back, those decisions often mark turning points in our lives that shape forever the people we become. Have you ever had the urge to laugh when you look back at the choices you made? Is there any point where you laugh at God now and wonder what God could possibly want from you? What would your response be if God asked you, "Why did you laugh?"

Are you at a point of being able to let go of the need to control everything in your life and let God lead you to wherever you need to be led?

The Prayer of
THE WOMAN WHO LAUGHED AT GOD

My Dear God,
When I was young, you surprised me with the love of my life
and then told us we had to move to find another home.
When I was more than a few years married
you surprised me with an inability to have children
and strengthened our love for each other.
When I was old, you surprised me with the promise
    of another life
and gently scolded when I laughed at all your surprises.
Keep surprising me, Lord,
for your surprise and my laughter keep me young
and full of life and full of love
and full of the knowledge in my deep heart
that, impossible as it might seem,
where you are is home for me.
Amen.

What is your prayer to God about the surprises in your life?

THE WOMEN WHO LOVED THE SAME SON

Now a man from the house of Levi went and married a Levite woman. The woman conceived and bore a son; and when she saw that he was a fine baby, she hid him for three months. When she could hide him no longer she got a papyrus basket for him, and plastered it with bitumen [tar] and pitch; she put the child in it and placed it among the reeds on the bank of the river. His sister stood at a distance, to see what would happen to him.

The daughter of Pharaoh came down to bathe at the river, while her attendants walked beside the river. She saw the basket among the reeds and sent her maid to bring it. When she opened it, she saw the child. He was crying, and she took pity on him, "This must be one of the Hebrews' children," she said. Then his sister said to Pharaoh's daughter, "Shall I go and get you a nurse from the Hebrew women to nurse the child for you?" Pharaoh's daughter said to her, "Yes." So the girl went and called the child's mother. Pharaoh's daughter said to her, "Take this child and nurse it for me, and I will give you your wages." So the woman took the child and nursed it. When the child grew up, she brought him to Pharaoh's daughter, and she took him as her son. She named him Moses, "because," she said, "I drew him out of the water."

EXODUS 2:1–10

||||||||||||||||||||||||||||||||||

The Backstory

From one perspective, Exodus is a story (some would say one of *the* stories) about the intervention of God in human history. From another perspective, it is also a story of religious differences. Pharaoh thought he was God, and God disagreed.

In either case, the story picks up where Genesis leaves us. Joseph, the son of Jacob, and all his people are in Egypt because a great famine had swept over the land of Canaan. Joseph, who had been sold by his brothers into slavery, years before had risen to a position of some power in Pharaoh's court and so was able to ease the passage of his people in this foreign land. But after some very prosperous times (and fruitful ones for the Hebrew people), Joseph died, thus setting the stage for the next events. "Then a new king, who knew nothing of Joseph, came to power in Egypt." (Exodus 1:8)

With these fateful words, the story of the Exodus begins to unfold and becomes, for both synagogue and church, the archetypal story of the deliverance of God's people from the power of oppression and the establishment of God's covenant with them.

For Jews, the story is retold at every Passover and it is told in such a way that it makes clear it is not our ancestors, but "we" who were brought out of the land of Egypt to enter into a covenant with God and become a nation.

For Christians, the story of God's deliverance means a deliverance from the power of sin and evil. Death is vanquished, and God reigns forever. A new covenant is written, confirmed in the blood of Jesus. We tell this story at the Easter Vigil as part of the salvation history leading to the story of Jesus' resurrection. We see, in that resurrection, the power of God at work in human history once again.

Just before this passage, which tells about the birth of Moses, we hear more closely the command of the unnamed king (some think he is Ramses II). His anger and fear that the Hebrews might become too powerful fuel a decree to kill all the male children, an act that amounted to a death sentence for a people.

We watch as unnamed women defy him at nearly every turn. First, midwives engage in a little bit of passive aggression. Drawing on their own compassion and love, they refuse to kill the baby boys of the Hebrews.

Then, even in the face of such deadly decrees, a Hebrew woman, a Levite, marries and gives birth to a child (both decidedly life-giving and also defiant actions) and then moves to save him from destruction. She puts him in a little "ark" (the word is the same as the one used for Noah's boat), where he floats on the flooded Nile to the unnamed daughter of the king, who raises him as her own child, even enlisting the help of the baby's mother without knowing it. Because of the love of these two women, Moses grew to adulthood.

What Does This Story Tell Us?

Almost always, in the telling and retelling of the Exodus, the stories of all those who conspired to thwart Pharaoh's plan to kill the sons of Israel become incidental, if they are mentioned at all. In popular culture, we can thank filmmakers Cecil B. Demille (*The Ten Commandments*) and even Steven Spielberg (*The Prince of Egypt*) for giving us a little glimpse of Pharaoh's daughter and Moses' sister and mother, but even they move quickly past them to get to the main plot. And they give us no glimpse at all of the midwives who refuse to kill the newborns. In the process, they overlook some wonderful additions to our understanding of God.

Mothers have been known to do just about anything for their children. The Hebrew woman and her husband were slaves and had no power in Pharaoh's Egypt. In the face of her child's certain death, she first hid him and then did the only thing she could think of that would save him. She let the river carry him to what she hoped was a less chaotic and more life-giving place.

By contrast, the king's daughter had remarkable privileges both as a woman in Egypt and as a member of the royal house. Drawn to the cries of an infant, she drew him out of the water. She must have known of her father's decree, but still she chose to save the Hebrew child's life, to name him and love him as her own child, and to find a nurse for him.

Mother love comes in all shapes, sizes, and colors, and the desire to give a better life to our children than we ourselves had runs deep, whether we are poor or rich, privileged or not. We have also seen what happens when such love is absent and where the spirit of a child is killed long before the body follows.

Where is God in this story? We know that the midwives disobeyed a king and risked their own lives to do what they thought was right (a more contemporary parallel would be those who hid Jews from Hitler's army during the Holocaust.) We are told that God "built up families" for them and gave them what Pharaoh would have taken away (Exodus 1:21). But God does not appear in the story of Moses' birth and adoption, nor will he until Moses is grown.

When we look at Moses' mother and Pharaoh's daughter, however, we can catch a glimpse both of the way God loves and the way God loves through us. In Moses' young life, love was characterized by the movements of these two women—movements of letting go and drawing out.

So, too, do we experience God's love. God's divine love in creation drew order out of chaos until the fruit of that love took shape and became a world that was good. God's redemptive love lets go of power and control.

God emptied himself as surely as Moses' mother emptied her hands of the ark that carried him; and both did this so that someone else could have life and have it abundantly. God's love does not force us to follow or love in return, but lets us go so that we might, in freedom, return to him.

But, just as powerfully, God's love draws us out of whatever chaos we might have encountered. It draws us out from values and priorities that culture or peer pressure might establish and sets us on a different path until, at the very end, we find that we have become one with God.

"Letting go" and "drawing out" are two expressions of our love for family and friends as well. Sometimes we have to let go of others so that they might become their own selves or find their own ways. And sometimes we have to draw them out and let them know that we are deeply, gracefully, wonderfully bound by love to them, to God, and to everyone.

ılıllılıllılıllılıllılıllılıllı

Meditation for Groups or Individuals

The wealth in the story of Moses' mother and the Pharaoh's daughter lies not just in their mutual love for the child, but in the different ways they reflect and demonstrate their love. For many of us, a mother's love is firm ground on which to stand and from which to venture out to see the world.

When the story of Moses' childhood is told in the Acts of the Apostles, it is three short sentences long: "At this time Moses was born, and he was beautiful before God. For three months he was brought up in his father's house; and when he was abandoned, Pharaoh's daughter adopted him and brought him up as her own son. So Moses was instructed in all the wisdom of the Egyptians and was powerful in his words and deeds." (Acts 7:20–22)

In this short passage, we can almost hear the love of Moses' mother, "Isn't this the most beautiful baby you have ever seen?" And we witness the love of his adoptive mother, who saw to it that her son had the best that Egypt had to offer. This is what God wants for us. He wants us to know that we are beautiful, and "precious in [his] sight, and glorious" (Isaiah 43:6, NAB) and that we can have the best God has to offer—even his own Son.

For us, God is both willing to let go of everything so that we can find our way and willing to draw us out of a flood with bonds of love so that we can make our journey home again.

Read the story again and meditate on these questions:

Where in your life have you let a person go because you loved him or her so much? When has someone let you go?

When have you drawn someone out of himself or herself or out of a dangerous place and set him on solid ground in love and care? When have you been drawn out by someone else?

Has there ever been a time when you have risked something in order to do what you felt was right?

Whether we know it or not, free will is an expression of God's love for us. God knows that love cannot be forced and, if not freely chosen, it is not love. When we choose to turn away from God, God lets us go. But God is always ready to draw us out if we just cry out. Can you name a time in your life where you turned away from God? Can you name a time when you felt the presence and the love of God draw you out and give you peace? What happened as a result of those times?

The Prayer of
THE WOMEN WHO LOVED THE SAME SON

God in heaven, you must know what it is to be a mother.
You know how love creates life and lets go
   so that life might flourish.
You know how such letting go feels (and sometimes is)
   a little bit like death.
You know too the joy of loving the child in all of us,
   who are drawn out of mother's wombs
kicking and screaming and looking for the love
   of parents and friends;
looking for your love as we make our way in a world
that is sometimes wonderful and sometimes threatens
   to drown us.
We give you thanks for the love that forms and shapes us
   and the love that saves us from all that would do us harm.
Keep us always in your love and when we wander away from you,
   gently let us go until we know that only in you
   will we find our rest,
then draw us up and out, safely to the home you have
   prepared for us.
Amen.

*What is your prayer to God about the way God lets you go
and the way God draws you out?*

*What would you say to God about your experience of letting go
and drawing out others?*

THE WOMAN WHO DEMANDED ACTION
FROM GOD

One day Elisha was passing through Shunem, where a wealthy woman lived, who urged him to have a meal. So whenever he passed that way, he would stop there for a meal. She said to her husband, "Look, I am sure that this man who regularly passes our way is a holy man of God. Let us make a small roof chamber with walls, and put there for him a bed, a table, a chair, and a lamp, so that he can stay there whenever he comes to us." One day when he came there, he went up to the chamber and lay down there. He said to his servant Gehazi, "Call the Shunammite woman." When he had called her, she stood before him. He said to him, "Say to her, Since you have taken all this trouble for us, what may be done for you?"...She answered, "I live among my own people." He said, "What then may be done for her?" Gehazi answered, "Well, she has no son, and her husband is old." He said, "Call her." When he had called her, she stood at the door. He said, "At this season, in due time, you shall embrace a son." She replied, "No, my lord, O man of God; do not deceive your servant." The woman conceived and bore a son at that season, in due time, as Elisha had declared to her.

When the child was older, he went out one day to his father among the reapers. He complained to his father, "Oh, my head, my head!" The father said to his servant, "Carry him to his mother." He carried him and brought him to his mother; the child sat on her lap until noon, and he died. She went up and laid him on the bed of the man of God, closed the door on him, and left. Then she called to her husband, and said, "Send me one of the servants and one of the donkeys, so that I may quickly go to the man of God and come back again." He said, "Why go to him today? It is neither new moon nor sabbath." She said, "It will be all right." Then she saddled the donkey...[and] set out, and came to the man of God at Mount Carmel. When the man of God saw her coming, he said to Gehazi, his servant, "Look, there is the Shunammite woman; run at once to meet her, and say to her, Are you all right? Is your husband all right? Is the child all right?" She answered, "It is all right."

When she came to the man of God at the mountain, she caught hold of his feet. Gehazi approached to push her away. But the man of God said, "Let her alone, for she is in bitter distress; the LORD has hidden it from me and has not told me." Then she said, "Did I ask my lord for a son? Did I not say, Do not mislead me?" He said to Gehazi, "Gird up your loins, and take my staff in your hand, and go. If you meet anyone, give no greeting, and if anyone greets you, do not answer; and lay my staff on the face of the child." Then the mother of the child said, "As the LORD lives, and as you yourself live, I will not leave without you." So he rose up and followed her. Gehazi went on ahead and laid the staff on the face of the child, but there was no sound or sign of life. He came back to meet him and told him, "The child has not awakened." When Elisha came into the house, he saw the child lying dead on his bed. So he went in and closed the door on the two of them, and prayed to the LORD. Then he got up on the bed and lay upon the child, putting his mouth upon his mouth, his eyes upon his eyes, and his hands upon his hands; and while he lay bent over him, the flesh of the child became warm. He got down, walked once to and fro in the room, then got up again and bent over him; the child sneezed seven times, and the child opened his eyes. Elisha summoned Gehazi and said, "Call the Shunammite woman." So he called her. When she came to him, he said, "Take your son." She came and fell at his feet, bowing to the ground; then she took her son and left.

II KINGS 4:8–37

The Backstory

Throughout the books of Kings, the stories of the prophets are woven in and out of the narrative, providing a witness to the divine power present in those dedicated to God. In these stories, Elijah and Elisha take their places as the first significant prophets independent of the monarchy and the priesthood. Unlike many of the other prophets, they are miracle workers, demonstrating the power of God. They also fulfill their roles by calling the king and his followers to faithfulness and obedience to the covenant.

Their message is not always welcome, nor are they always successful. Elijah shows up in I Kings 17 and immediately performs two miracles. He multiplies food in a famine and he raises a young boy from the dead and restores him to his mother, who acknowledges that he is a man of God. At the end of Elijah's prophetic ministry, he (literally) passes his mantle to Elisha, whom many recognize as the heir apparent to Elijah.

The story of Elisha and the Shunammite woman, as well as two stories of miraculous abundance (an oil jar that fills every vessel brought to it and twenty barley loaves and fresh ears of grain that feed a multitude), provide the proof that the power of God now rests with Elisha. New Testament scholars often draw parallels between these miracle stories and those performed by Jesus. Because of stories like the feeding of the 5,000 (Matthew 14:13–21) and the raising of the widow's son (Luke 7:11–16) or Lazarus (John 11:17–44), Jesus is clearly identified as a man of God or a prophet like Elijah and Elisha. "Who do people say that I am," Jesus asks Peter in Matthew 16. "Some say John the Baptist and others Elijah..." Peter answered.

And what of the woman? As Elisha dines at her house, her intuition that he is a holy man grows. The priority of hospitality in the region is apparent in the care she takes to make Elisha feel comfortable. He has his own space in the couple's house, something similar to being made a member of the family.

The fact that she has no children means at least two things. The family line and name will cease after she and her husband are dead and, if she outlives her husband, there will be no one to take care of her in her old age.

Widows were among the marginalized groups in Israel. They could not hold property; nor did they have a means to support themselves. Based on the number of passages commanding the opposite, it would also seem that they were treated harshly at times. Thus, they depended on the care of others.

The law and prophets make special mention of the responsibility of Israel to care for widows and orphans along with other disenfranchised groups, and God is named as the protector of widows (Psalm 68:5). Still, the Shunammite woman displays confidence in her situation, noting simply that "she lives among her own people," when Elisha asks what he might do for her. "I have everything I need," she seems to say.

What Does This Story Tell Us?

It is not very often that confident and competent women are presented in the stories of Scripture. Esther and Judith are two; the Shunammite woman is another.

Though she is married, she is the main character in this household, directing her husband and servants with equal ease. She is also something of a risk-taker. She travels to Elisha with only her servant, taking care even to saddle her own donkey. When Elisha gives an inadequate response—giving his staff to his servant, Gehazi, and telling him to go to the house—the woman gives her heartfelt response: "I will not leave without you."

Subtly we might hear her saying: "You are not sending your stick to my dead son; he and I deserve better; we deserve your presence." Or, as the old proverb has it: desperate times call for desperate measures.

The Shunammite woman is any of the people we know, male or female, who live lives of quiet dignity every day. These are the people who look for ways to help others and for ways to make those around them feel at home.

They are the friends who will take it upon themselves to go to great lengths to help those they love or to correct an injustice. They will demand the best for family, for friends, and even for strangers. And they would travel a great distance if they thought they could save someone by doing so.

In many ways, through her welcoming manner toward Elijah, in her persistence in the face of tragedy, and in her demand that the holy man be present and walk with her to return to her dead son, the Shunammite woman bears some resemblance to more contemporary women and men who insist that the business of hospitality and love toward family and strangers is the occupation of us all.

Think of Catholic Worker founder Dorothy Day, who demanded that those in authority pay attention to the poor and the homeless. And when she was ignored, she persisted. Today, thirty years after her death, hundreds of Catholic Worker communities worldwide continue to thrive.

When the Shunammite woman defied convention to correct wrongs, she took a risk to correct the wrong. What other people come to mind in this same regard? Many will recall Oskar Schindler, who spent his entire fortune to save over 1,000 Jews during the Holocaust, only to die penniless himself. We might also think of Archbishop Oscar Romero, who sacrificed his life by demanding—from the pulpit—international intervention to protect victims of the then-corrupt El Salvador government.

And there are, among us always, countless men and women who give their all to help others and provide hospitality for everyone. They go to great lengths to correct injustice. They demand the best for family, for friends, and even for strangers.

What does the Shunammite woman teach us about God? Certainly, one thing we know is that God creates us with a tremendous capacity for courage and strength in the face of devastating setbacks.

Time and again in natural disasters, good people have stepped up to help neighbors, friends, and families rebuild shattered lives and find the courage to go on living. Not every life is saved, but every life is counted as worthwhile. Every life is deemed worthy of rescue, and loved ones will not rest until every effort has been made. But we also know something else.

When we listen to her voice and her insistence that Elisha return with her to her home, we can hear the voice of God, who pushes us—despite our imperfections or our lack of imagination, or our belief that something less would do—to do what is right and to present our whole selves to those in need.

In God's eyes, we are all counted worthwhile; we are all worthy of the best—so much so that when God sojourned on earth, he mounted his donkey and rode to his death that we might be given new life. When we consider that, it is easier to see how the saints, both named and unnamed, had the courage and strength to do what they did. And it is easier to imagine how we might do that as well.

|||||||||||||||||||||||||||||||||

Meditation for Groups or Individuals

In the story of the Shunammite woman, three beacons of imagination stand out. The first involves her hospitality to Elisha. She thinks about this guest room and what it should contain. An old Celtic rune of hospitality (a proverb with mystical meaning) encourages people to welcome the stranger or wayfarer by putting food in the eating place, drink in the drinking place, and music in the listening place. She decides on a bed, a table, a chair, and a lamp: a place to rest, to eat or write or build, to meditate or pray, and to see when the way is dark. When I think of these items, I wonder if we have need for anything else.

Another place for our imagination is in the woman's reaction to her son's death. She does what needs to be done and goes to Elisha. She does not hesitate. She does not wonder whether she should go or not.

The power of her belief and the passion of her love compel her to seek out the one she thinks is a holy man. We do not know if she knew of his other miracles. We do not know what she took with her. We do know that she would not leave without him.

Her faith is our encouragement and our inspiration. In grief or sorrow, we are not helpless. We can demand that God be with us regardless of the outcome. But we also remember that God can demand the same of us, with as much persistence, passion, and love as the Shunammite woman showed.

Finally, the last sentences beg another look. "...[Elisha said to her], 'Take your son.' She came and fell at his feet, bowing to the ground; then she took her son and left." Where would she go after that? This was a gift of new life. How would it change her life forever?

Read the story again and meditate on these questions:

Has there ever been a time when you have displayed or been the recipient of unusual courage, compassion, or care? Describe that moment.

Is there someone in your life right now who needs the attention of God and others? Have you demanded it?

Have you made Christ welcome in your house as a regular visitor? How have you furnished the "guest room?"

Have you ever had a God-given miracle in your own life?

Jesus gave us a gift of new life in his passion, death, and resurrection. How have you shown your gratitude? When you took the gift of new life from Jesus and left the room, where did you go?

The Prayer of
THE WOMAN WHO DEMANDED ACTION FROM GOD

My Lord, I don't know what you thought you were doing.
　　I prepared a place for you in my heart
　　I looked for your coming and looked forward to your
　　　　visit
And I was satisfied with all you had given me
　　I did not require anything else.
And then you promised me the world—and delivered it
　　Howling into my hands; breaking open my loving
　　　　heart
And I gave my love freely to child as to husband.
Even when you took the child, I loved him
　　Loved him enough to go and demand his life from
　　you and your holy one.
Dear Lord, how many other women have made a place
　　for you and for love in their homes and in their hearts?
What new life are you holding for them and for the world?
And when will they receive it?
　　Amen.

*Write your prayer to God about the new life in you and the
things in your life for which you demand that God be present.
If you have time, write a little about how God demands your
presence.*

LOVERS

I asked a few friends to tell me what they thought of when I said the word, "lovers." They started with the common and particular like *Romeo and Juliet*, and said that when we first think of lovers, we think immediately of romantic images of Central Park in the spring or the joy of young love, or our first crush. But then they began to call out words and phrases almost faster than I could write them down: relationship, companionship, embrace, desire, being filled, lifting up, safety, risky, heat….Every bit is precious.

These are the words we might apply to many kinds of love, and indeed, the conversation turned to love itself in an instant with examples of spousal love, parent-child love, the love of brothers and sisters or good friends, and the love of God. One thing seemed clear. We all had many different experiences of love and the "lovers" in our lives had lifted us up, protected us, challenged us, given us warmth and comfort, and had filled out hearts with joy.

One of the first things we learn as children in church is that God is love. We might spend our whole lives pondering what that means. We also know that if we are made in the image of God, then we, too, are lovers in the broadest and best sense of the word, and we reflect God best when we enter into a deep relationship of love with God, family, the best of friends, with one other person, or a community of persons. There are many different ways of being a lover, and most of us experience more than one at a time.

For all of us, to be a lover is to want the best for the other; to be a lover is to share the profound secrets of heart and soul and to be willing to shape and be shaped by the other. (Some of us will also share the secrets of the body gently and intimately.) To be a lover is to see the face of God in all we meet and to be the face of God to all we meet. To be a lover of any kind is to be a constant reminder and example of the presence of God in the world.

The lovers of these stories are both everything we might expect and nothing like we expect when we first hear the word. Two of them love each other, body and soul, and they will express their love and delight in words completely inadequate to the task. One loves her family and is an example of the lengths to which we will go and the risks we will take on for those we love. The last will give her love to a new member of the family because of the loving trust she has placed in another. All of them can be our teachers.

THE LOVERS WHO WERE HEAD OVER HEELS

Woman:

My beloved is all radiant and ruddy,
    distinguished among ten thousand.
His head is the finest gold;
    his locks are wavy,
    black as a raven.
His eyes are like doves
    beside springs of water,
bathed in milk,
    fitly set.
His cheeks are like beds of spices,
    yielding fragrance.
His lips are lilies,
    distilling liquid myrrh.
His arms are rounded gold,
    set with jewels.
His body is ivory work,
    encrusted with sapphires.
His legs are alabaster columns,
    set upon bases of gold.
His appearance is like Lebanon,
    choice as the cedars.
His speech is most sweet,
    and he is altogether desirable.
This is my beloved and this is my friend...

SONG OF SONGS 5:10–16

Man:

How graceful are your feet in sandals,
   O queenly maiden!
Your rounded thighs are like jewels,
   the work of a master hand.
Your navel is a rounded bowl
   that never lacks mixed wine.
Your belly is a heap of wheat,
   encircled with lilies.
Your two breasts are like two fawns,
   twins of a gazelle.
Your neck is like an ivory tower.
Your eyes are pools in Heshbon,
   by the gate of Bath-rabbim.
Your nose is like a tower of Lebanon,
   overlooking Damascus.
Your head crowns you like Carmel,
   and your flowing locks are like purple;
   a king is held captive in the tresses.
How fair and pleasant you are,
   O loved one, delectable maiden!
You are stately as a palm tree,
   and your breasts are like its clusters.
I say I will climb the palm tree
   and lay hold of its branches.

SONG OF SONGS 7:1–8

The Backstory

The Song of Songs belongs neither to the Law nor the Prophets, but to the third category of Hebrew Scripture: the Writings. Of these, Job, Psalms, Proverbs, Ecclesiastes, Song of Songs, Wisdom and Sirach (Ecclesiasticus) are referred to as the Wisdom literature by Christians for their use of traditional wisdom forms and their emphasis on the Wisdom of God, traditionally portrayed as a woman.

Jack Miles, in his book, *God: A Biography*, points out that God is notably silent in the writings. There are no great acts (like creation or the exodus), and there is only one occasion in which God utters a word: his great speech toward the end of the book of Job.

Instead, the people who inhabit these stories and the wisdom literature in general must rely on their memories and past experiences of God to help them make sense of the world around them. They observe and comment on all of creation as they move through it. Every experience becomes another opportunity to learn about God from the life they live and the world that they make their home.

Thus, when they remember God in times of trial, more often than not they are comforted and given the grace to move on. When they experience times of prosperity, they relate it to God, who gives every grace from heaven. Even if things go horribly wrong, the constancy of God is not in question and some, like the psalmist, can still demand his presence or make him a target of blame (as in Psalm 88).

The Song of Songs, with its sexual imagery and unconventional poetry, was one of the last books accepted into the Hebrew canon. There was no theology of covenant or chosen people or monotheism here. In fact, God is not mentioned at all. The entire book is a love song between two people who take delight in each other and, in a way, all creation. In a Bible where the women are often silent, Song of Songs highlights the woman's feelings and words—she has about twice as many lines as her partner. (Some speculate that the book was attributed to Solomon to offset this emphasis.) Those wondering about its inclusion in the canon asked: "What does the poetry of lovers have to do with God?" And, "Who can be serious when you are comparing the best attributes of your beloved with things like doves and gazelles and giraffes anyway?"

In the early Church, the inclusion of the Song of Songs in the canon was justified by looking at it allegorically. Clearly, thought the scholars, the man and the woman of the poetry corresponded directly to God and his people. Spousal imagery was often used to describe that relationship in other parts of Scripture, though rarely in such earthy and sexual terms. More contemporary interpretations are inclined to hear this as it is—a love song between two people that also engages the religious imagination as we think about our relationship with God.

<hr>

What Does This Story Tell Us?

Sometimes, our emotions are so strong that words fail us. Only can past experience help to describe what is presently right in front of us. What these two passionate lovers have experienced is a created world that is full of beauty, joy, delight, laughter. Facing the one they love, they can only rely on their former experience to help describe this new one. And so they use the most beautiful, most lively things they can think of to describe the one they love.

Ravens, doves, jewels, lilies, palm trees, spices, and the color purple all lend the lovers words to talk about their beloved. These common and uncommon objects become the language of love because, where love exists in any form, there is no adequate language to describe it.

Even now, expressions of endearment (the French "My little cabbage [*ma petite chou*]" or the English *sweetie pie*) lift up the common and make them extraordinary. The lovers of Song of Songs use the glory of creation to describe their beloved. Do they not honor God, who created all things, when they do that?

When we use the ordinary and the beautiful things of the world to describe the people we love, we recognize that all of creation, especially the creation of human beings, reveals the love of God.

In the Creed we confess: "I believe in God the Father almighty, Creator of heaven and earth…" Those words express our understanding that the world is wonderfully and lovingly made by a God who cares for us. If we do not reflect on that every now and then, we are missing the boat. If we are not touched by the notion that God loved the world into being we might also miss the fact that loving one another in whatever relationship we are in is what makes us most like God.

And love that touches the bottom of the heart and soul sometimes reduces us to babbling and to comparisons that don't make any sense to those on the outside, but just might make all the sense in the world to the lover who uses them.

When my future husband came home to meet my family (driving six hours to stay for 12 hours and then driving six hours back the next day), I said goodbye to him and returned to the room I shared with my sister. After a little while she said, "Why are you smiling," and I couldn't answer her. I could only grin more.

When my daughters were born and I looked into their eyes, I felt an overflowing peace and joy, giving them loving personal nicknames and marveling at the tiny features and the smallest movement.

Love that touches the heart cannot be expressed exactly in words. The best we can do is smile and laugh and compare this love to what we know in the world and it comes nowhere near to what we mean any more than ivory towers are necks, or legs are alabaster columns set on gold. But it is the only way we can try to describe the way he/she makes us feel and delights our eyes and our desire to become one with our beloved.

We are God's beloved ones, and the generative power of God's love babbled words that created the world and brought us the incarnation, Jesus, as the loving Word of God. Jesus, God incarnate, did not compare us to fawns or gold, but called us children of God and friends, and he died on the cross for us.

When Jesus came, his followers had no words for him either. The love he had shown them and the love they had for him rendered their language inadequate, so they had to search their experience to see if there were any words to use for this encounter.

They found something close in the stories of their ancestors and the promises of God that they had heard from them. They listened anew to the message of the prophets and they gradually began to think of Jesus in the words of their experience—as redeemer and servant, as savior of the world and messiah.

They called him the Son of God and the Word of God who was there when God first loved the world into being.

And one writer—his name was John—listened, reflected and finally wrote the only thing that made sense: God is love. God, the lover, said he wanted to be one with us, not because we were so great or so beautiful, but because he loved us. Bathed in that love, we are as beautiful as anything on earth could ever be.

Meditation for Groups or Individuals

We might spend a lifetime pondering John's simple phrase, "God is love." What does that mean for us? How have we experienced love in our own lives?

The love of parents for children and children for parents is most often unconditional and nurturing and completely challenging. Parents are overwhelmed by the responsibility to this small person in their care and children develop nearly singular devotion for their parents as they look to them for almost every need.

Friends experience a different love that shares support, care, and a kick in the pants when deserved.

The love of spouses for one another adds the dimension of the erotic, caring not only for the heart and mind, but also for the body of the other. Their desire sees beauty not only in what is perfect, but also in what is not, for they recognize that not any one thing, but everything put together in this one person is beautiful.

Finally, self-giving love, what the Greeks called *agape* and the Hebrews *hesed*, seeks only the good for the beloved, submitting even to death if it means saving another's life.

If we are sure of nothing else in our lives, we can be sure that we are called to be in a relationship of love with God. Deuteronomy 6:4 (and Jesus, who lifted up the commandment as the first and greatest) commands that we love God with all our hearts and all our souls, and all our strength.

Every love that we experience somehow reveals God's love, and every time we love someone else, we reveal ourselves as the image of God. For us, God is a lover who takes delight in the beauty of creation, and in us—even though we are not perfect. God is also a parent who nurtures and cherishes, and a friend who supports and makes us strive to do better. And God emptied himself for us that we might live forever with him.

Read the passage from the Song of Songs again and reflect on these questions:

What are your "terms of endearment" or comparisons for those you love? What do those words reveal to you about the love of God?

Imagine how you might describe God and how God might describe you if the two of you were expressing your love for one another. What words would be used?

How do you describe your relationship with God at this moment? What various forms of love has it shown? How has it changed over time?

How do you show your love for someone else? How do you show it for God?

What are some of the ways you deepen your love for someone else or for God? Is it important to do that?

The Prayer of
THE LOVERS WHO WERE HEAD OVER HEELS

God of my heart,
When you loved the world into creation,
it was our beginning, for without your love we would not be.
So fill our hearts with love even now
    that in every place we wander, love will spill out and overflow,
    planting itself in places of dark and hurt and making them
    fruitful again.
Make us so generous with your love
    that every person we encounter
    may have evidence that you are in this world.
Help us see that in your love we are beautiful
    and that where beauty is there is your love
    poured out and brimming over until at last the whole world
    finds itself beloved and praising you.
Amen.

Write a prayer to God about your understanding of God as a lover who is in love with all creation.

RAHAB, THE LOVER WHO SAVED TWO SPIES

Then Joshua, son of Nun, secretly sent out two spies from Shittim, saying, "Go, reconnoiter the land and Jericho." When the two reached Jericho, they went into the house of a harlot named Rahab, where they lodged. But a report was brought to the king of Jericho that some Israelites had come there that night to spy out the land. So the king of Jericho sent Rahab the order, "Put out the visitors who have entered your house, for they have come to spy out the entire land." The woman had taken the two men and hidden them, so she said, "True, the men you speak of came to me, but I did not know where they came from. At dark, when it was time for the gate to be shut, they left, and I do not know where they went. You will have to pursue them immediately to overtake them."

Now, she had led them to the roof, and hidden them among her stalks of flax spread out there. But the pursuers set out along the way to the fords of the Jordan, and once they had left, the gate was shut. Before the spies fell asleep, Rahab came to them on the roof and said: "I know that the LORD has given you the land, that a dread of you has come upon us, and that all the inhabitants of the land are overcome with fear of you. For we have heard how the LORD dried up the waters of the Red Sea before you when you came out of Egypt, and how you dealt with Sihon and Og, the two kings of the Amorites beyond the Jordan, whom you doomed to destruction. At these reports, we are disheartened; everyone is discouraged because of you, since the LORD, your God, is God in heaven above and on earth below. Now then, swear to me by the LORD that, since I am showing kindness to you, you in turn will show kindness to my family; and give me an unmistakable token that you are to spare my father and mother, brothers and sisters, and all their kin, and save us from death."

"We pledge our lives for yours," the men answered her. "If you do not betray this errand of ours, we will be faithful in showing kindness to you when the LORD gives us the land." Then she let them down through the window with a rope; for she lived in a house built into the city wall. "Go up into the hill country," she suggested to them, "that your pursuers may not find you. Hide there for three days, until they return; then you may proceed on your way." The men answered her, "This is how we will fulfill the oath you made us take: When we come into the land, tie this scarlet cord in the window through which you are letting us down; and gather your father and mother, your brothers and all your family into your house. Should any of them pass outside the doors of your house, he will be responsible for his own death, and we shall be guiltless. But we shall be responsible if anyone in the house with you is harmed. If, however, you betray this errand of ours, we shall be quit of the oath you have made us take."

"Let it be as you say," she replied, and bade them farewell. When they were gone, she tied the scarlet cord in the window. They went up into the hills, where they stayed three days until their pursuers, who had sought them all along the road without finding them, returned. Then the two came back down from the hills, crossed the Jordan to Joshua, son of Nun, and reported all that had befallen them. They assured Joshua, "The LORD has delivered all this land into our power; indeed, all the inhabitants of the land are overcome with fear of us."

JOSHUA 2:1–24 (NAB)

||||||||||||||||||||||||||||||||||

The Backstory

Before Moses died, he handed over leadership of the Hebrew people to Joshua, his young apprentice. Joshua had accompanied Moses and the people out of Egypt and was commander of the army in the first battle against the Amalekites. Since Moses would die before they reached the Promised Land, it was Joshua who would lead the people in the conquest of Canaan.

For many, the stories of the conquest are difficult to read because the invading Israelites are under divine order to destroy the inhabitants of the land. The Israelites' conquest of Canaan is told two different ways. The book that bears Joshua's name, from which our story is taken, recounts a swift and decisive conquest.

The book of Judges, which immediately follows, suggests that the Promised Land was settled over a much longer period of time, with many more roadblocks and battles. No matter how it happened, it seems clear that the people believed that God guided them and would ultimately take care of them. They do not seem concerned with the fate of the people they displace. This makes our story all the more remarkable.

The story of Rahab takes place just before Joshua goes into battle. Joshua wants information about Jericho, and sending spies seemed the best way to do it. The spies ended up staying in what some scholars describe as a public house.

We know nothing of Rahab except for the word used to describe her in Scripture. It is the Hebrew word for harlot or prostitute. Such women were tolerated but marginalized in Israelite society. They used their bodies to make enough money to put food on the table and a roof over their heads.

Since our story mentions Rahab's father, mother, and brothers, we might imagine that she is supporting them or paying off a family debt in the only way she can.

In general, women could not own property, nor do we hear of them taking jobs; thus if there was any money owed or payment to be made, women had little choice about how they earned it. Neither the ancient Israelites—nor many of us today, if we are honest about it—could expect much good to come from them.

And yet, Rahab, the prostitute, hid the spies from the king of Jericho at great risk to herself. Rahab, who might have been rewarded much better by the king had she betrayed her visitors, chose to defy him.

Rahab believed that the God that these strangers worshipped was Lord of heaven and earth. She had no reason to think that the strangers would treat her well—very few others did and they were an invading army—but still she asked only that they spare her family when the time for conquest came (which they did in chapter 6).

Among the significant features of this story are the stalks of flax that are spread out on the roof indicating that it is close to Passover and the scarlet cord which Rahab hangs from her window so that the Israelites will not harm her family. The color suggests the blood of the Passover lamb, which the Israelites put outside their doors so that the angel of death would pass over them, leaving them safe.

What Does This Story Tell Us?

Certainly some people might object to including a prostitute among the "lovers" who can teach us about God or about ourselves. And yet, Rahab's deep love for her family is evident in her willingness to do what she must in order to support them and keep them together.

Among her own people, she was scarcely better than a slave, and she undoubtedly worked hard to pay off whatever debt had been incurred. Her reputation as a prostitute, colors and shapes the way she is perceived by all those around her. Even her lifesaving deed becomes suspect in that light. But look more closely at this woman who saved the life of two spies and helped an army in the process.

Rahab is in the right place at the right time. We have no idea what led the two spies to her house. Maybe they thought they could learn something; maybe they thought they could hide out since she was a person on the fringe of society. Or maybe they wanted a moment of intimacy, even with a stranger, before turning back to battle preparations.

In any case, the immediacy with which the spies came to her suggests another force at work. She cannot know of the God of Abraham, Isaac, and Jacob, but she has heard of his power and has come to believe in him. She knows that he is God in heaven and on earth. Neither the king of Jericho, nor the gods of the Canaanites are a match.

Finally, when the possibility of escape confronts her, she does not think of herself first, but of her father and mother and brothers and sisters. She names her entire family before she thinks of herself. She wants them to be safe above all.

What kind of love must it take to shun personal safety in order to save others? Rahab is a model for anyone who lives a life of quiet dignity in almost unlivable circumstances.

Many people are defined and judged by what others call them, but this woman, scorned as a prostitute, never forgot that even strangers deserve hospitality, and we are called to save the lives of all who are in danger. She shows all of us that being a lover in the broad sense of the word sometimes means sacrificing a little bit of ourselves in order to make a better life for others. Rahab also reminds us that God sometimes chooses to work with and through the ones we might judge as wholly inadequate.

Thankfully, God is not bound by our standards. Rather, God loves us all, seeks out whatever is good in us and uses it to show the world the Divine Presence. In Joshua 6, we learn that this marginalized Canaanite woman and her family are brought out of Jericho to live in the midst of Israel. No longer marginalized, her actions made family out of an enemy.

In later centuries, tradition identified Rahab with the mother of Boaz (who married Ruth) in Matthew's genealogy of Jesus (Matthew 1:5)—though some scholars question whether this is the same person.

Additionally, the anonymous writer of the Letter to the Hebrews would praise Rahab's faith and tell the world that she "did not perish with the disobedient because she received the spies in peace" (Hebrews 11:31).

We say faith is a gift. If so, God gifted Rahab with everything that faith could offer: the knowledge of God's power, the desire to do good for her family and for others, and the strength and courage to live her life with integrity, no matter how marginalized by society.

And when the time came, she did not betray that gift, but she asked that her family be spared before she herself was. She may not have been able to name the love of God in her life, but she surely knew it in her heart, and she showed it to all she met.

||||||||||||||||||||||||||||||

Meditation for Groups or Individuals

When most of us think about lovers, we do not usually add prostitutes to the list. There is no love in selling one's body for money, and very few of us can transcend our distaste to look at the person behind the act.

We rage against the existence of prostitution rings and pay little attention to the economic situations that lets them thrive. Rarely do we stop and realize that prostitutes are also children of God and beloved.

Prostitutes may have families whom they cherish and try to help any way they can. Certainly many women around the world feel forced into prostitution by circumstances beyond their control. They believe they have no other choice.

This story challenges us to look at our "blind sides." Can we see the love in someone whom we dismiss as indecent or unworthy? Can we accept that this person may be just as faithful (or more so) than we ourselves? Can we believe that God cares for them as openly as he cares for us and is able to work through them to make himself known in the world?

Rahab is a woman whose care and love for her family may have placed her in a dire situation. Is she a lover? All over the world, women and men have taken on jobs they would rather not have had because they loved and cared for families who needed them.

They have made what they could, sold what they could, did their best to put a little food on the table and probably eked out a subsistence living doing it. In the midst of that, it would have been very hard to think about anything else.

So when one such person can care about the lives of two strangers along with her own, we might, perhaps, pause for a minute and look carefully—at her capacity to love and at ours. As Christians, we might also remember that Jesus once said: "Truly I tell you, the tax collectors and the prostitutes are going into the kingdom of God ahead of you." (Matthew 21:31)

Read the story again and reflect on the following questions:

What have I been willing to give up (or take on) for someone I love? Would I be willing to do what Rahab has to do?

What are my blind sides? In what way have I marginalized people whom I judge unworthy of God's time or effort or mine?

Have I ever met a person who could teach me nothing about love or anything else? Why did I think that?

For what or whom would I be willing to risk my life?

The Prayer of
RAHAB, THE LOVER WHO SAVED TWO SPIES

Lord, my God
I would rather be doing something else
But my family needs me and food is necessary.
Every day, I think about the strangers I have seen
and loved the best I could, though the loving felt hollow
and forced—not like me at all.
Still I am a child of God, your Child
Still I am made for love and in love's image
And I do love, powerfully and deeply.
Still your voice stirs in my heart and
  your power is ever before me.
Lift your hand and save me from despair and sadness
And help me find a home filled with love
  in the midst of your people,
    my family safe beside me.
Amen.

  What is your prayer to God about the life and the love
  you are living right now?

THE LOVERS WHO WERE
GREAT-GRANDPARENTS TO A KING

When she was back with her mother-in-law, Naomi said to her, "My daughter, I must seek a home for you that will please you. Now is not Boaz, with whose servants you were, a relative of ours? This evening he will be winnowing barley at the threshing floor. So bathe and anoint yourself; then put on your best attire and go down to the threshing floor. Do not make yourself known to the man before he has finished eating and drinking. But when he lies down, take note of the place where he does so. Then go, uncover a place at his feet, and lie down. He will tell you what to do." "I will do whatever you advise," Ruth replied. So she did just as her mother-in-law had instructed her.

Boaz ate and drank to his heart's content. Then when he went and lay down at the edge of the sheaves, she stole up, uncovered a place at his feet, and lay down. In the middle of the night, however, the man gave a start and turned around to find a woman lying at his feet. He asked, "Who are you?" And she replied, "I am your servant, Ruth. Spread the corner of your cloak over me, for you are my next of kin." He said, "May the LORD bless you, my daughter! You have been even more loyal now than before in not going after the young men, whether poor or rich. So be assured, daughter, I will do for you whatever you say; all my townspeople know you for a worthy woman. Now, though indeed I am closely related to you, you have another relative still closer. Stay as you are for tonight, and tomorrow, if he wishes to claim you, good! Let him do so. But if he does not wish to claim you, as the LORD lives, I will claim you myself. Lie there until morning." So she lay at his feet until morning, but rose before men could recognize one another. Boaz said, "Let it not be known that this woman came to the threshing floor."

Then he said to her, "Take off your cloak and hold it out." When she did so, he poured out six measures of barley, helped her lift the bundle, and left for the city. Ruth went home to her mother-in-law, who asked, "How have you fared, my daughter?" So she told her all the man had done for her, and concluded, "He gave me these six measures of barley because he did not wish me to come back to my mother-in-law empty handed!" Naomi then said, "Wait here, my daughter, until you learn what happens, for the man will not rest, but will settle the matter today."

RUTH 3:1–18 (NAB)

IIIIIIIIIIIIIIIIIIIIIIIIIIIIII

The Backstory

The book of Ruth, with its tale of friendship and family bonds, is a great example of a Hebrew short story. While the story itself is set in the time of the judges of Israel before the monarchy is established, there is evidence to suggest that it was written much later.

An Israelite man from Bethlehem had taken Ruth, a Moabite, as his wife when the Israelites went to Moab during a famine. When her husband died, Ruth chose to return with her mother-in-law, Naomi, to Israel.

When Naomi asks why she would ever want to do such a thing, Ruth speaks the line for which she is most remembered (and which shows up in more weddings than we can count): "Wherever you go, I shall go; wherever you lodge, I shall lodge…" Ruth and Naomi go to Israel to make a home for themselves. It was hard work.

Widows (as has been noted) were often a marginalized group who held no property and were thus dependent on the community. Still, Naomi and Ruth did the best they could.

In Israel, they gather grain in the field of Boaz, who is the near relative of Naomi and thus a potential husband for Ruth (Levirate law stated that the nearest relative, usually the brother, of a dead man had the duty of marrying his widow and fathering a child to bear the name of the deceased).

Along with many of the women in the Old Testament, Naomi is clever and practical. She knows that "home" includes the care of her extended family and making sure that her daughter-in-law is able to have children (and to raise up a family for her dead son).

So Naomi urges Ruth to lay her claim on Boaz. On the threshing floor, Ruth does so.

Boaz, an honorable man, makes sure that there is no impediment to a marriage. (A closer relative would have had the right to marry Ruth if he had so desired).

As soon as he knows it is all right to do so, Ruth and Boaz marry. Ruth bears a son named Obed, who would become the father of Jesse. The son of Jesse was King David. From the line of David, the Messiah would be born in Bethlehem.

While the relationship between Ruth and Naomi is a primary focus, the acceptance of Ruth, a foreigner, by Boaz is just as striking. The love between Ruth and Naomi and between Boaz and Ruth gives Ruth a particular pride of place as part of God's salvific plan—ancestor to a great king and named by the evangelist, Matthew, as one of the four women in the genealogy of Jesus (Sarah, Rahab, and Mary are the others).

In the biblical canon for Christians, Ruth is placed after the book of Judges (presumably because of the time frame). In the Hebrew Bible, it is part of the Writings (Kethubim) and, as such, occupies the latter part of the Hebrew canon between Song of Songs and Lamentations. Once again, God is not a prominent figure in the Writings. Instead, the reader relies on experience and memory to reveal God's presence in the world.

What Does This Story Tell Us?

In this particular passage, Ruth shows Naomi that she trusts her implicitly, while Ruth and Boaz uncover (figuratively and literally) their attraction for each other.

Ruth had already experienced his compassion and kindness firsthand, and made no protest to Naomi's plan to become one family with him as his wife. He is impressed by her care for her mother-in-law, and by her virtue and her beauty.

As their coming together unfolds, we are also swept up in a story which gives meaning and makes sense of both the good times and the bad times of the main characters and sees them all as part of God's action.

The journeys of Ruth, Naomi, and Boaz are exactly like those in our lives where, only in hindsight, can we look back and say, "That was the hand of God. But I did not know it at the time." In a closer look, we might also see the many places in which love and the cooperation with God's dream for us are found.

The yearning for a place to belong is foundational to all of us. We call it home: the place we are accepted for who we are and the place where we can reveal our deepest needs.

When Ruth accompanied Naomi back to Israel, she was saying that Naomi was family and she trusted that even a foreigner would be welcome. For her part, Naomi recognized the importance of home and belonging for Ruth, and thus begins their plan.

Naomi loves Ruth and sees that Boaz can give both of them a home. Ruth is sent to the threshing floor at the end of a hard day's work for both of them—Boaz in cutting the fields and supervising the workers and Ruth in gathering what was left over for her and Naomi.

The threshing floor is where everything comes together. The chaff is separated from the wheat and the wheat is ground into flour for bread. There, the workers eat, drink, and sleep after a hard day's labor. And it is in the dark of night that they awake to whatever else they need, whether they know it or not.

Ruth comes to the very place where the fruit of the day's labor is revealed so that she can see what fruit will come from the plan she and Naomi make.

When Boaz wakes to find her lying beside him, his surprise turns to delight. He knows the woman he sees there. He knows that she has worked hard to support her mother-in-law and that she is caring and loving. He also sees in her the desire to make a home with him—a place where both of them can belong. He recognizes his own need for love and, immediately understanding the possibility in this plan, he takes on this extended family with joy.

Our quest for God and for companionship starts with a yearning for home as well. "Why did God make me?" the old catechism asked. "God made me to know, love, and serve him in this world and be happy with him in the next." We need a place to belong and the desire for love and for God seems built into us. St. Augustine called it a thirst. Others simply call it longing for home.

To get there, we might have to follow Naomi and Ruth and travel far from where we started, and we might need the company of others—friends and family or even complete strangers to strengthen us on our way.

Like Ruth, we may have to work hard in a strange place out of love for the ones who brought us here. Like Boaz, we may have to be open to what lies right in front of us and see in it the possibility of real grace.

Both Ruth and Boaz eventually made their way to the threshing floor and so too must we, either because someone has called us there or we have been drawn by a force we do not know. But it is on the threshing floor that we will make our desire known to God and to ourselves.

Threshing floors come in all shapes and sizes. They are the places we work and eat and take our rest. They are schools, offices, neighborhoods, homes, and churches.

Our threshing floor is any place in which the fruit of our labor and the needs of our bodies and souls are made manifest in the light of day and the dark of night.

Here we name our need for home and know it as the place where we are loved. Here we realize that the love God poured into our souls at the beginning finds its best expression in the love of others and in loving God, the one who made us.

So it should be no surprise that these threshing floors are the places where, when we least expect it, we wake up to find that God has laid down next to us and has called us to become one with him forever.

Or perhaps it is we who have found a place next to God, revealing our desire for love and our need to belong to the divine household. In either case, God takes hold of our hearts, tenderly offers the love of family and helps us extend that love to others—the fruit of labor of a different kind.

If we learn one thing from the story of Ruth and Boaz, it is that holy plans are often worked through human desire and need, and that these same elements inform God's own design. Seeking and finding a place to belong, to be loved, and to love can bring us home in a way we never thought possible.

Meditation for Groups or Individuals

When we were young and before we were married, my husband and I would talk about the houses we grew up in and the house we wanted when we grew older.

I can still remember the description of our dream house. It had a large kitchen with room for gathering and a big front porch for summer evenings. I wanted a stream running through the house with a small waterfall, if possible.

Our reality is very different. The kitchen is small; the stream non-existent; the front porch is adequate. It bears little resemblance to the grand plan, but we raised our children here with love and humor. And their friends seemed content to talk and laugh in the small living room with great bowls of fruit salad made with love. It was a place they felt cared for, a place they could belong without too much effort.

If there was a threshing floor in our lives where work and play, love and desire came together, this was it. When I think back on the laughter, the heartache, and the sharing that occurred on this threshing floor, I find myself in awe, thinking: "Surely God was here in this place, and I did not always know it." Whether it was God who uncovered us there or the other way around, I know that somehow we belonged together with God in that place.

The fruit of our love may not be the Messiah, but may well be the place where others can see the presence of God in our midst. In the end, love makes a home and makes us at home where we let God into the deep recesses of our hearts and we turn to one another to express that love as best we can.

Read the story of Ruth and Boaz again and reflect on the following questions:

Where do you feel the most sense of belonging? Why?

In the story, Ruth makes a bold move to stake a claim on the love of Boaz. Have you been bold enough to go after what you wanted (or needed) to make you happy? What were the circumstances of that?

What is the threshing floor in your life? Where and to whom do you reveal your desires and longings for home and love? How has God been present there?

What would you say to God about your longing for anything? What would you say to God about the needs of your heart?

Do you think God ever expressed his longing for you? When and how?

The Prayer of
THE LOVERS WHO WERE
GREAT-GRANDPARENTS TO A KING

God of my heart and my heart's desire,
I do not always know the place where you have brought me
Nor do I always know the faces of those around me.
But I think I know your love when I see it
    and your care when it is shown to me
    in the love and compassion of another
Help me to see you whenever and in whatever way
    you come to me;
Help me to find the place where I can uncover my heart to you.
For only in opening my heart can I make a home
    for you, Love itself in our midst.
And only when I am at home in your love can I truly belong.
Amen.

What would you say to God about the love that has come to you?
Where have you encountered that love most often?

PRIESTS

A careful look at priests today reveals men (and women in some denominations) who have taken a vow to live public lives of holiness and prayerful leadership. One priest I know described his ministry of teaching, preaching, and leading as "pointing to Jesus and getting out of the way." It took up most of his day. Another said: "It is a great privilege to serve God and his people."

While few of us are called to ordained priesthood, every one of us is baptized into the priesthood of all believers, sharing in the mission of Jesus Christ as priest, prophet, and king. We take on the challenge to live our lives as a public witness to the transforming power of grace.

We are called to worship God and to be the face of Christ to every person we encounter. We are to carry the gospel into our everyday lives and live out the message of good news. And in a compelling way, we are called to account for our actions and hold others accountable as well. We can only ask God to give us the grace we need for so great an honor.

The priests in these stories are teachers, preachers, and leaders. In the fine tradition of all priests today, they wear multiple hats, and each is known for being something besides a priest.

One is a mysterious figure, a king as well, who wanders out of nowhere in the story and into an encounter with Abram, but the memory of his action informs and shapes the psalmist, the letter to the Hebrews, and the priests of today.

Another does double duty as a prophet and, almost more than any other, accepts his mission to watch for the Lord and to call himself and others to account for their actions. His understanding of the word of the Lord is both a challenge and a comfort to a wayward flock.

The third is also a scribe who hears his community cry out for the ground of their identity and puts people in touch with the law of God in the depths of their hearts. In so doing he helps them see where God is. The lessons from these stories just might help us all be better at our own priestly behavior, wherever and however we serve that out.

THE PRIEST (AND KING) OF GOD MOST HIGH

Then one who had escaped came and told Abram the Hebrew, who was living by the oaks of Mamre the Amorite, brother of Eshcol and of Aner; these were allies of Abram. When Abram heard that his nephew had been taken captive, he led forth his trained men, born in his house, three hundred eighteen of them, and went in pursuit as far as Dan. He divided his forces against them by night, he and his servants, and routed them and pursued them to Hobah, north of Damascus. Then he brought back all the goods, and also brought back his nephew Lot with his goods, and the women and the people.

After his return from the defeat of Chedorlaomer and the kings who were with him, the king of Sodom went out to meet him at the Valley of Shaveh (that is, the King's Valley). And King Melchizedek of Salem brought out bread and wine; he was priest of God Most High. He blessed him and said, "Blessed be Abram by God Most High, maker of heaven and earth; and blessed be God Most High, who has delivered your enemies into your hand!" And Abram gave him one tenth of everything.

GENESIS 14:13–20

‖‖‖‖‖‖‖‖‖‖‖‖‖‖‖‖‖‖‖‖‖‖‖‖‖‖

The Backstory

Coming toward the beginning of the "Abraham Cycle" of stories in Genesis, this chapter is something of an anomaly. Its beginning suggests a historical narrative replete with kings of countries, contrasting allegiances, and invasion plans. Within the chapter, our story of Melchizedek stands apart. How did we get here?

When Abram (who would become Abraham) and his wife, Sarai (who would become Sarah) were called by God to leave their homeland of Ur, they journeyed south for a time with their nephew, Lot. They stopped near Shechem and then Bethel, where Abram built an altar.

When famine hit that area, they went a little further to Egypt and stayed there until the famine ended, gradually returning to Bethel. By that time, the flocks and herds belonging to Abram and Lot were large and they did not think there was enough room for both of them. Lot went left into Sodom and Abram went right into the land of Canaan. Unfortunately, the kings of the surrounding area attacked Sodom and captured all the people, including Lot, and took possession of all their goods.

When our story opens, Abram goes to rescue his nephew and returns triumphant, not only with Lot, but with all the people and their possessions. Predictably, the king of Sodom does him the honor of coming out to meet him, perhaps to thank him and celebrate the victory.

Then they both encounter the mysterious priest-king of Salem who, until this point, has never been mentioned. It is worth noting, though, that Salem, while never positively identified as Jerusalem, is certainly linked to the city of David at times (see Psalm 76:2) and the word suggests *shalom*, which means peace.

Melchizedek's name may mean *the king of righteousness* or *Zedek is my king*, but in the history and imagination of Israel became linked with the Davidic messiah who establishes righteousness and peace (Psalms 72:1–7 and 110:4).

Finally, the valley of Shaveh (which means even) is thought by some to be the Kidron Valley, which separated the city of Jerusalem from the Mount of Olives.

What Does This Story Tell Us?

I can only imagine the joy of a king and a people who have been rescued from an oppressor by a champion. Abram was the champion in this story, and the meeting between him and the king of Sodom must have been a memorable one, certainly a celebration to be marked with joy.

In our country and culture, such occasions often include food and drink, good friends, and late nights. Abram and the king of Sodom may have already begun their festivities when Melchizedek, the priest-king of Salem, inexplicably appears and brings another dimension to this encounter. His bread, wine, and blessing suggest a ritual which places "God Most High" squarely at the center of the celebration and in a way that future generations remembered when they started thinking and longing for the coming of the Lord.

In doing this, Melchizedek makes God the focal point of our lives—whether we are celebrating the most joyous of occasions or weeping in deep anguish.

He also demonstrates the significance of rituals, which indicate the "thin places" of the world where God breaks in and makes us aware of the divine Presence that is always and everywhere around us. (*Thin Place* is a Celtic idea that proposes that there are places and times where the door between the secular and sacred worlds is so thin that God could—and does—break through at any time.)

In his brief appearance in Scripture, Melchizedek embodies the basic characteristics of priests and kings. As king he's an example of obedience to God. As a priest, he offers praise and sacrifice to God at all times. (His name is invoked at ordinations of priests.)

While most of us are not priests or kings, our acceptance of the call to be disciples of Christ challenges us to follow his example to make God the center of our lives and to respond to God with obedience and prayer.

‖‖‖‖‖‖‖‖‖‖‖‖‖‖‖‖‖‖‖‖‖‖‖

Meditation for Groups or Individuals

Often, the trouble with reading stories about people of ancient times is that we must transcend the distance of time and space in order to become part of the story.

Since we rarely find ourselves facing death to rescue a relative from the hands of an oppressor, Abram's circumstance in this encounter may not mean much to us.

But when we do daily battle (in small ways) against temptations, bad habits, and those who would bring us down by their actions, then we *can* imagine what Abram, the king of Sodom, Lot and his family, and all those captured in the attack must have felt: a mixture of joy, relief, absolute fatigue, and the feeling of a burden lifted from their hearts and minds.

Certainly there was gratitude for Abram for destroying the enemy and a sense that they had found a champion. In imagining those emotions, we can also remember times when we have felt joy or relief, those times when fatigue has threatened to overcome us, or when we have been so thankful for someone's kindness or intervention.

These moments of high and low, peak or valley are times when our perceptions of God's presence or absence are at their most acute. Melchizedek reminds us that God is always present, always knowing our joy and our anguish, always ready to accept our anger, happiness, and cries that we are too tired to go on.

Melchizedek also lets us know that God is our "table companion." The ritual of bread and wine begins first by setting tables in any place and at any time that people gather together in friendship and prayer. This is what shapes us as a people of God.

All of those moments, rituals, prayers, and memories of God's presence come together when we gather at Mass as a community of faith. There, we encounter the great sacrament. Jesus uses the common elements of bread and wine to give himself, body and blood, to his people. When that happens, we know God is always with us.

Read the passage again and reflect on the following questions:

What are the high and low places of your life and how have you felt God's presence or absence in them?

Just as the kind of day you have experienced shapes how you come to your dinner table, the kind of life you have experienced shapes

how you come to the Eucharistic table. Reflect on what you
"bring to the table" and how it helps or hinders your full
participation in the Eucharist.

Are you comfortable in asking God to make you more aware
of his presence? Are you comfortable in telling God that you need
to feel the Divine presence more in your life?

How do you "set the table" for God in your life?

The Prayer of
THE PRIEST (AND KING) OF GOD MOST HIGH

You are holy, Lord, my God.
in my deep joy and in my deepest sorrow
You alone are worthy of praise and thanksgiving
   in the valley of delight or the shadow of death
You only, Lord of all, are the companion of my life
   in the hours of my waking day
and for the length of sleeping (and sleepless) nights.
Let me praise you with prayer and song and work well done
   all of which you have given me;
Let me praise you with service to the poor and love to all
   strengthened by your love for me
Let me praise you with gathering around the table in love
   with bread and wine, broken and poured out
   with an offering of self—yours and mine
   wholly given, wholly shared
Until I am wholly sent, ready to praise you and call on you
   in every place and at every table that you are.
Amen.

How do you pray to God, who is present in the center of all we do?

THE PRIEST WHO LOVED THE LAW OF GOD

All the people gathered together into the square before the Water Gate. They told the scribe Ezra to bring the book of the law of Moses, which the LORD had given to Israel. Accordingly, the priest Ezra brought the law before the assembly, both men and women and all who could hear with understanding. This was on the first day of the seventh month. And Ezra opened the book in the sight of all the people, for he was standing above all the people; and when he opened it, all the people stood up. Then Ezra blessed the LORD, the great God, and all the people answered, "Amen, Amen," lifting up their hands. Then they bowed their heads and worshiped the LORD with their faces to the ground. Also Jeshua, Bani, Sherebiah, Jamin, Akkub, Shabbethai, Hodiah, Maaseiah, Kelita, Azariah, Jozabad, Hanan, Pelaiah, the Levites, helped the people to understand the law, while the people remained in their places. So they read from the book, from the law of God, with interpretation. They gave the sense, so that the people understood the reading.

And Nehemiah, who was the governor, and Ezra the priest and scribe, and the Levites who taught the people said to all the people, "This day is holy to the LORD your God; do not mourn or weep." For all the people wept when they heard the words of the law. Then he said to them, "Go your way, eat the fat and drink sweet wine and send portions of them to those for whom nothing is prepared, for this day is holy to our LORD; and do not be grieved, for the joy of the LORD is your strength." So the Levites stilled all the people, saying, "Be quiet, for this day is holy; do not be grieved." And all the people went their way to eat and drink and to send portions and to make great rejoicing, because they had understood the words that were declared to them.

NEHEMIAH 8:1–2, 5–12

ıııııııııııııııııııııııııııı
The Backstory

When the Babylonians took Israel into exile in the latter part of the sixth century BC, they destroyed the temple in Jerusalem and removed all the able-bodied men and boys from the country.

Gone was the center of worship; gone was the seat of political power in the king. The southern kingdom of Judah (all that remained of the 12 tribes of Israel) ceased to exist as a political entity and the spirituality of the people began to falter badly.

When Cyrus of Persia freed the Israelites from Babylon, they returned to a place that did not remember them. Familiar landmarks and ways of life had vanished in the forty or so years of their exile. The only thing binding the Israelites together was the memory of their identity as a covenant people of God. But with no temple in which to worship, even that small comfort seemed inadequate.

In this milieu, the books of Ezra and Nehemiah tell about events that occurred from about 538-400 BC. Nehemiah is the governor of Judah and Jerusalem. Ezra is identified as both a priest (a descendant of Aaron) and a scribe (an interpreter of the law) who accompanied the people home from Babylon and returned the sacred vessels to the ruined temple. Ezra 7:10 tells us that "Ezra had set his heart to seek the law of the LORD and to do it, and to teach in Israel statutes and ordinances."

In the narrative of these books, the two oversaw the rebuilding of the temple as a place of worship and a focal point of Israelite life, giving the returning exiles a sense of belonging and a visible community of faith. After the building of the temple, the walls of Jerusalem were erected with the temple at its center.

On the first day of the seventh month, Ezra (who was considered by later rabbis as a second Moses) gathered the people and brought out the book of the Law to read. Scripture records that the people wept at hearing the words they thought had been lost to them.

The books of Ezra-Nehemiah are usually considered one literary piece and belong to the Writings in the Hebrew Bible. While the events depicted in them are questioned by scholars (and often historically contradicted in other books of Scripture) the story gives a theological emphasis to the centrality of God's law in the midst of the people, and the importance of remaining faithful to God. Here, we turn to the experience of this priest and people, the examples of their faith (or lack of it), their trust in God, and their own observations to teach us about God and ourselves.

What Does This Story Tell Us?

In countries in which religious freedom is suppressed, the faithful of all religions bear great personal risk to gather and worship as their faith dictates. Such gatherings are often referred to as "underground" churches because of their hidden nature.

In every century (even today) underground churches in oppressive countries continue to operate despite threats of punishment and even death. An outsider looking in might say such commitment is foolish, but that outsider cannot know the power of a covenant with the living God.

In this story, the people of Israel had been exiled for a long time from the center of their lives in God. Worship in a foreign land was undoubtedly difficult, if not impossible. Adherence to the demands of the covenant was broken down in the reality in which they lived.

The return to Jerusalem was an occasion of great joy and greater questions: Who are we now? How are we a people of God today? In truth, every generation in every church might ask that question, particularly when faced with scandal or dwindling congregations or just the busyness of everyday life.

In this passage we get a glimpse of a congregation—priest and people—actively seeking the word of God for their answer. Ezra, who has kept the law not only alive in his heart, but also physically present in the books he returns to the Jerusalem temple site, listens and responds to the people whom he is leading.

The Israelites articulate their desire to hear the words that mark their identity as a covenant people. At the first glimpse of the book of the Law being opened, the people stand up, a sign of the thirst to take the Law not only into their minds and hearts, but also into their bodies as well. In this one gesture, the oldest and the youngest (those old enough to understand) expressed their willingness to hear and obey.

In this, they are like us when we stand to show respect and admiration for someone or to make a point with emphasis. Ezra blesses God, the people assent, and in that context of shared prayer, Ezra (with his helpers) proclaims the Law and gives sense to it, so that everyone could understand.

In the dance between congregation and priest, we glimpse what is necessary to know ourselves as God's people even if we have forgotten most of what that means and everything around us has changed.

First, there must be someone to guard our story. Storytellers can be anyone who remembers that we are called by God to live in covenant with God forever. Frequently they are the priests among us—indeed, that is one of their charges, but they may be any pastoral leader or elder who articulates the vision of faith and keeps hope alive. Every congregation needs storytellers.

Second, we have to name our need to remember our origins and our story so that we might once again embrace the freedom of God's children.

Third, we must be willing to give our whole selves to the effort. Being a child of God and a disciple is not only an intellectual assent, but an assent of the body and soul as well.

Fourth, we must come to God with gratitude, blessing him for all we have been given. Here the storytellers and the listeners join together to give thanks.

Finally, we must all be teachers who help give sense to the words of God and we must all be learners who listen and understand. There is always more to know. Those who teach most often also need to learn, and those who learn can teach others.

The passage tells us that the people learned the Law with understanding and they wept when they heard it. Ensuring that we know and understand the words of God is a sign of saints and scholars. Grasping how central God is to the heart of our lives touches us in every part of our being.

The people of Israel wept because they thought they had lost their identity as people of God. When they heard Ezra proclaim it, they remembered and rejoiced. And they did one more thing which we would do well to follow: they shared what they had with those "for whom nothing is prepared." We have to wonder whether it was only food and drink they shared. Perhaps they shared their experience as well.

Whether we identify ourselves with the priests or congregation or both in this passage, Ezra and the congregation of Israel show us how to place the story of our relationship with God and the sign of our faith at the center of our identities and homes.

With patience and love, they proclaim, listen, and share the word. These are the demands of the priestly mission of Christ to which all of us are called by baptism. For those who are in ordained ministry, they are the foundation of a life given in public ministry to God and God's Church.

Meditation for Groups or Individuals

Coming Home is a phase that evokes memories of Christmas dinner and summer vacation, of visiting relatives and getting in touch with neighbors and friends we have not seen for a long time. *Coming Home* is the anticipation of familiar sights, smells, and sounds and also the anxiety that things have changed; and that neither we nor the people or places we remember are ever going to be quite the same. Both those realities are true.

There is the joy of rediscovered comforts *and* that we are different people than we were the last time we were here. We also know that there is something about home, wherever that may be, that puts us in touch with who we are at a deep level.

To be at home is to be in the place where we can be most authentically ourselves. Here our deepest relationships reveal themselves, our great ideas surface, and we feel safe enough to uncover and tackle those things that get in our way—the demons who whisper, "You are not loved…you are not good enough…you will never find your way."

When we are far from home, we lose our sense of who we are and where we come from. We lose sight of the source of our strength.

The creation story of Genesis tells us that we are made in the image of God. If home is the place we can be most ourselves, it makes sense then to say that our home is any place where God is present and where we are awake to that presence.

But sometimes we need a reminder of who we are. What is the mirror where we can see ourselves transformed by the love of God? For the Israelites, that mirror was the Law, the faith they practiced, which was given in love by God as a sign of God's covenant with them.

For Christians, the mirror is the life of Christ and the practice of his twin commands to love God with all our heart, soul, and mind and to love our neighbors as ourselves (both taken from the Pentateuch and part of what the Israelites would have heard in our story).

The experiences we've had, the people we have met, and the places we have gone have shaped us in ways we have not yet discovered, but at our core, we remain the image of God and beloved. When we come home to faith and the practice of it as adults, we might carry a lot of the same anticipation and anxiety we do when we return to a childhood home: What if this is not for me? What if I cannot find God or myself here? What if there is no more than what I see?

With the Israelites of a more ancient time, we come back to the faith of our lives—some every week, some every year, and some after many years and wonder if this is home for us. We may hope that some things remain the same and others will be different. And we know that we have changed and the faith of our childhood no longer serves us well as adults. Who are we now in God's eyes? How do we find that out? The questions make us hungry for more knowledge and a deeper relationship with God.

What could we read or hear that would ground us in our identity as people of God? What is the core of our faith? Every Sunday we recite the Creed and hear the Gospels. Maybe now is the time to stand up, opening ourselves, body, mind, and soul to learn again what God has done for us and prepare to be filled with a relationship that both comforts and challenges.

Maybe now we can come together as one with our priests in the service of the Lord. Now is the time to ask questions, wrestle with answers and know that we are on this path together, believing that God walks with us. In that understanding, we can worship and serve and share the celebration with all those for whom nothing has been prepared.

Read the passage again and reflect on the following questions:

What feels like home for you today? What grounds you most?

Is there a Scripture reading or a statement of belief that presents the core of your faith today? What is it?

Has there been any time in your life when you have felt "at home" in the presence of God? Has there been a time when God has seemed far away.

How much of your identity is tied up with your belief in God?

Do you come to church with expectation and joy? Why or why not? If not, what would it take to make those feelings happen?

Has your faith changed from childhood to adulthood to (if applicable) "the wisdom years?"

Can you imagine what it would be like to weep with joy on hearing the priest or other minister read the words of the Gospel?

The Prayer of
THE PRIEST WHO LOVED THE LAW OF GOD

I am yours, Lord, and you are Mine
And yet there are times when I feel lost and unsure
Though others tell me who I am to them
   I do not know who I am to myself or to you
Though I cling to prayer and to the book
   I seem closed to your voice in my ear
   and your love in my heart.
Let me hear your words stirring on the wind in deserted places.
Let me know surely in mind and body, in heart and soul
that I am Beloved, a child of God
made when your loving Word first troubled the waters
and later decided to stay awhile
Let me weep at the memory of a life lived
   in the newness of creation
   and the waters of rebirth and in the words of the Spirit
And then, Lord, knowing who I am as if for the first time,
In service and celebration, let me go out and invite others
   to the joy of being known and known as Yours.
Amen.

Write your own prayer about finding home in God.

THE PRIEST WHO WAS A PROPHET

Then the spirit lifted me up, and as the glory of the LORD rose from its place, I heard behind me the sound of loud rumbling; it was the sound of the wings of the living creatures brushing against one another, and the sound of the wheels beside them, that sounded like a loud rumbling. The spirit lifted me up and bore me away; I went in bitterness in the heat of my spirit, the hand of the LORD being strong upon me. I came to the exiles at Tel-abib, who lived by the river Chebar. And I sat there among them, stunned, for seven days.

At the end of seven days, the word of the LORD came to me: Mortal, I have made you a sentinel for the house of Israel; whenever you hear a word from my mouth, you shall give them warning from me. If I say to the wicked, "You shall surely die," and you give them no warning, or speak to warn the wicked from their wicked way, in order to save their life, those wicked persons shall die for their iniquity; but their blood I will require at your hand. But if you warn the wicked, and they do not turn from their wickedness, or from their wicked way, they shall die for their iniquity; but you will have saved your life. Again, if the righteous turn from their righteousness and commit iniquity, and I lay a stumbling block before them, they shall die; because you have not warned them, they shall die for their sin, and their righteous deeds that they have done shall not be remembered; but their blood I will require at your hand. If, however, you warn the righteous not to sin, and they do not sin, they shall surely live, because they took warning; and you will have saved your life.

EZEKIEL 3:12–21

ıııııııııııııııııııııııııııııı

The Backstory

On first glance, Ezekiel is known more for being a prophet than for being a priest. His book is one by three major prophets (Isaiah and Jeremiah are the others), with the bulk of his writing relaying the message of the Lord to Israel during and just after the exile.

The visions that open his book—the living creatures covered with wings and the wheel within a wheel—are the stuff of dreams (or nightmares) and belong more to apocalyptic imagery than to prophecy.

Much of the divine revelation relates God's displeasure with Israel for idolatry and disobedience, the main reasons given for the exile. And certain small portions, such as the vision of God as shepherd (Ezekiel 34) or the vision of dry bones (Ezekiel 37), are filled with the possibility of new life after the exile, a life God promises to those who remain.

Like all prophets, Ezekiel is a medium for the word of God, acting out God's message in his own life. Ezekiel criticizes the leaders of the people for leading them astray. Included among those leaders were kings, false prophets, and even priests who misinterpreted the word of God to the people of Israel.

But Ezekiel himself is a priest, the first named priest and prophet of Israel. As priest, he was a cult figure, one who offered sacrifice and led worship. As prophet, he called out to the people to return to the Lord and pointed out where the Lord might be found.

Because he embodied these twin spheres of worship and return, Ezekiel became a figure of transition. In the period before the exile, priestly functions of sacrifice and worship were often under prophetic attack because they were done mechanically, with no thought or conversion of heart. Priests, in many ways, had ceased to represent the holy or to lead the people to an understanding of God.

When Babylon destroyed the temple in Jerusalem in 587 BC, the ministry of the priests was put into jeopardy, and the center of the religious practice of the people was taken away. Some forty years later, the people returned, desiring nothing more than restoration of the true understanding of priesthood and finding in the temple the foundation of their faith.

As priest and prophet, Ezekiel was a key figure in bringing both the authority of revelation and the priestly ministry of sacrifice and care for the people into the post-exilic period which would see the rise of priests as the leaders of the people.

In Ezekiel's vision of the new temple, he outlines the duties of the priests:

"They shall teach my people the difference between the holy and the common, and show them how to distinguish between the unclean and the clean. In a controversy they shall act as judges, and they shall decide it according to my judgments. They shall keep my laws and my statutes regarding all my appointed festivals, and they shall keep my sabbaths holy." (Ezekiel 44:23–24)

The passage at the beginning of this section comes from the beginning of the book, long before Ezekiel hears the word of God speak of an end to exile and a new hope for the people of Judah. Among the first things Ezekiel hears is a call to mission—one that would make any of us uncomfortable with its emphasis on personal involvement in the lives of others.

What Does This Story Tell Us?

Imagine what Ezekiel was thinking when he began preaching to the exiles in Babylon. I suspect all who were taken from their homes expressed some fear, hopelessness, or sorrow at the loss of their loved ones, and genuine questions about the future. Whether and when they would return to Judah was unknown. Who would lead them was also a question.

Meanwhile, those who were left behind (thought to be the women, children and those too old or weak to rebel) could only wait and wonder and get on with their lives as best they could.

Ezekiel's mission, both as prophet and priest, was to be a "sentinel" (other translations read: "watchman") to declare what God was going to do and then to rouse the people to the appropriate response—to turn from evil and stay the course for good. If he failed to warn them, Ezekiel would share their fate.

This call to be a "watchman" over others is antithetical to today's society. We are rugged individuals raised on multiple messages to mind our own business regarding other people's actions. "*I don't want to get involved...I don't know what to do...someone else will take care of it*," are among the many excuses that we use to avoid confronting someone about bad behavior.

Whistle-blowers are frequently ostracized, while stories abound about the professional "code of silence," which keeps members from one group or industry from turning in others in the same group. We are far better about engaging in good behavior and encouraging others to do the same, particularly when the occasion is global disaster—think about the response to the Indonesian tidal wave of 2004, Hurricane Katrina in 2005, and the 2010 earthquake in Haiti.

But God's mission to Ezekiel (and Ezekiel's response) dares us to do more. It dares us to enter a relationship of responsibility to and for one another. It dares us to be more aware of God's presence in the world and to call one another to respond by turning from evil and doing good for all people, not just in times of disaster, but in every moment.

To be a "watcher" in the mold of Ezekiel is not, as some might imply, to stand by while the world goes to hell in a handbasket, but to recognize that we are all bound together and accountable to one another and to God. To call others to holiness is to call ourselves to holiness as well.

God's mission to Ezekiel shows us it is not only what we do for ourselves that matters, but what we do for one another as God's people. If one falls, we are all the poorer for it; if one shows forth the grace and compassion of God and does what is right in God's eyes, we are all blessed by it.

Our common priesthood is marked by a mission to be watchers for and with one another. Vatican II puts it another way. "Each individual layman must stand before the world as a witness to the resurrection and life of the Lord Jesus and a symbol of the living God. All the laity as a community and each one according to his ability must nourish the world with spiritual fruits. They must diffuse in the world that spirit which animates the poor, the meek, the peace makers—whom the Lord in the Gospel proclaimed as blessed. In a word, "'Christians must be to the world what the soul is to the body.'" (*Lumen Gentium*, Dogmatic Constitution on the Church *38*)

As a prophet, Ezekiel's vocation was to call all people to faithfulness to the Law; as a priest, his responsibility was to make sure that each of them heard and understood God's revelation.

As a watcher, he had to do both—caring for the spiritual well-being of the people as he might care for himself, even if it meant preaching in season and out to some who did not want to hear. We do not always think about this aspect of priesthood—our responsibility to care for and about the spiritual welfare of others.

Even now, all priests are required to pray for those in their care each day, to preside at common worship, to teach the gospel, and to point out where God is and exhort everyone to follow.

They do publicly in the church what we are called to do in the world—always and everywhere to work and pray in the Spirit, always and everywhere to watch for the presence of God and, by word and example, urge others to turn away from sin and follow Christ.

Thus, we comfort those with whom we live and work and are counted among those who watch and walk with the people of God.

‖‖‖‖‖‖‖‖‖‖‖‖‖‖‖‖‖‖‖‖‖

Meditation for Groups or Individuals

When have you been a watcher? People watch over those who are sick, who are in trouble, or who are young. We watch as friends, as parents, and as spouses.

We try to navigate the boundary between caring for and taking control, urging the person silently, and sometimes loudly, to get well, get help, or grow up.

Parents are particularly keen to point out dangerous situations to their growing children in the hopes of helping them steer the right course. And they must affirm what the child does well.

Those who watch friends move into an unhealthy relationship struggle with whether to say something or not, reluctant to cause pain, but equally reluctant to wait for the inevitable and painful end.

In the community of faith, God watches over us and challenges us to watch out for one another. We are to be vigilant like a sentinel, observing where God is active in the world and seeing all the ways in which human freedom subverts God's desire for union with all creation; for the divine dream for one community of love that reflects God's glory.

We are also to look for the opportunities in which we can cooperate with the work of God to make the world a holy place. And we are to do all this as part of our "spiritual sacrifice"—the offering of ourselves for God's service.

To be a watcher has three movements.

First, the watcher looks to see. This looking is not a casual glance, but an openness to all that lies in front of us. We are frequently blinded by our own fear or need for power. When God calls us to look, there is only one focus and that is the presence and action of God in the world and in our lives. If we are distracted, we can easily miss it.

The second movement is to point to God wherever God may be found, and to let others see that it is God who calls out to them and offers a transformed life in service to the Divine.

The final movement is to stand with those who are around us and accept that our salvation is bound up with theirs, that in some measure, we rise and fall together. Sometimes on the journey to God, we have to pull each other along the way and carry those who are too weak to carry themselves. The path to God is not just about how I get there, it is also about how I helped my traveling companions make the journey as well.

Read the passage again and reflect on the following questions:

When you look at the world, where do you see God active, and what do you think God is saying to us?

Have you ever had to warn someone that his behavior was unacceptable and that he needed to change? What was that like for you? How do you think the other person handled it? Would you do it differently today?

Has someone ever challenged you about your behavior? What was your reaction? If this has not happened to you, can you imagine how you would react?

Jesus tells us that we are to love one another. What is the relationship between that and our responsibility for one another? Is there a point where we have to let the other person find his or her own path?

What is your own understanding of the mission to be a watcher or sentinel? Explain how you would connect your mission as sentinel with your baptism into the priesthood of Jesus Christ.

The Prayer of
THE PRIEST WHO WAS A PROPHET

My Lord, God
I want to know why.
Why did you pick me for this task?
    to watch and to warn
    to nudge and to shove people back into place
Why is that my particular mission today?
I have enough trouble keeping myself in line
    and watching for God in my life.
How do you expect me to point you out to so many others,
    when my own blindness can get in my way
    and my life is not the best?
But if this is your will, then give me your grace and eyes to see
    where you walk this earth
Give me your grace and a heart
    that shows forth your love to the world
Give me your grace and the will
    to follow those who watch for me
So that step by step we will walk together
    into the new day of your coming light.
Amen.

*Write your own prayer about the responsibility
to care for one another.*

PROPHETS

The word for prophet in Hebrew could mean either "one who is called" or "one who calls." Whether God calls the prophet to his or her task or the prophet calls the people to faithfulness and a return to God, the sense of mission and attentiveness to God's word is always there.

In a way, we "hear" God speaking in the books of the prophets and come to know what God cares about and challenges us to do. The phrase: "Thus says the Lord" shows up so frequently in prophetic writings that it is difficult to tell where the prophet stops and God starts.

People often refer to the prophets as the mouthpieces of God who present God's message in no-nonsense terms and warn of the consequences of failing to follow the word of God.

But it is important to know that the prophets also announce the good news of God's mercy and care for Israel and the vision of a world in which God's justice rules and all live in peace.

Prophets were drawn from their ordinary lives into an extraordinary mission which did not always make them beloved figures. Their vocation called for them to be particularly aware of what was going on in the world and the ways in which God was present.

Their mission was to call people to faithfulness to the covenant and law of God. Whether the prophets wrote a larger book with many chapters spanning several years (the major prophets) or wrote a smaller book encompassing a single incident or two (the minor prophets), or showed up in a few stories of the great history of Israel, each one gave a unique example of the challenges involved in responding to the call of God.

The age of the great writing prophets—which included names like Isaiah, Jeremiah, and Ezekiel—ended long before the time of Christ, but the world has always known people whose voices and actions have made us reach out and try to be better and more faithful servants of God.

However, as a people we are generally no better at following our modern-day prophets than the Israelites were at following the prophets of their day. Sometimes, as the saying goes, God just has to hit us "upside the head" with a two-by-four just to get our attention.

The three prophets we meet here are known, but not always liked, by the people to whom they preach. Their specific duties are varied—one is a traditional proclaimer of God's word, though it is not a peaceful one; one is asked to authenticate an antique found in the wall of the temple; and one is asked to anoint a king—twice.

Whatever their job at the time, these people do their best to reveal and interpret what they understand God to be saying to them. Their faithfulness is an example for us as well.

THE PROPHET WHO GOT A MESSAGE FROM GOD IN AN ART STUDIO

The word that came to Jeremiah from the LORD: "Come, go down to the potter's house, and there I will let you hear my words." So I went down to the potter's house, and there he was working at his wheel. The vessel he was making of clay was spoiled in the potter's hand, and he reworked it into another vessel, as seemed good to him.

Then the word of the LORD came to me: Can I not do with you, O house of Israel, just as this potter has done? says the LORD. Just like the clay in the potter's hand, so are you in my hand, O house of Israel. At one moment I may declare concerning a nation or a kingdom, that I will pluck up and break down and destroy it, but if that nation, concerning which I have spoken, turns from its evil, I will change my mind about the disaster that I intended to bring on it. And at another moment I may declare concerning a nation or a kingdom that I will build and plant it, but if it does evil in my sight, not listening to my voice, then I will change my mind about the good that I had intended to do to it.

JEREMIAH 18:1–10

The Backstory

In the late sixth century to mid-seventh century BC, between the Assyrian invasion that destroyed the northern kingdom of Israel and the Babylonian triumph that eliminated the southern kingdom of Judah, the people of Israel enjoyed a small period of prosperity.

It fell to Jeremiah, a prophet from the priestly family in Anathoth to preach repentance and change of heart for those who lived in and near Jerusalem at the time.

The vision of his call included an image of God's hand on him while he was still in his mother's womb and the understanding that God was going to make him "a fortified city" (Jeremiah 1:18) to stand against any invaders who would speak or act in opposition. It did not turn out to be an easy task.

Jeremiah was widely disliked for supporting the reforms of King Josiah and urging the people to follow the law of God. For this, he was arrested, jailed, and was thrown into a cistern (something like an open sewer) for his troubles.

The inhabitants of Jerusalem preferred to listen to Hananiah, another prophet, who preached a future that did not require giving up their habits and lifestyles. Unfortunately, the young king Zedekiah was influenced by such preaching and revolted against Babylon. As a result, the city was destroyed by King Nebuchadnezzar in 587 BC.

Among Jeremiah's more famous prophecies is the vision of a "new covenant" which God would make with the people (Jeremiah 31:31–34). In this covenant, the law of God would be carved in the hearts of all so that no one would have to rely on another to teach it. Jesus echoes the promise of the new covenant in the story of the Last Supper: "This cup is the new covenant in my blood, which shall be shed for you…" (Luke 22:20).

The passage we are reading comes a little over a third of the way into the book toward the end of Jeremiah's ministry under King Jehoiakim (609-598 BC). Jeremiah was one of the more introspective prophets who took time, every now and then, to reflect on his own life and what the call of the prophet meant. This is one of those moments.

|||||||||||||||||||||||||||||||||

What Does This Story Tell Us?

An old school friend was looking for a class to take at the college we attended. As she read over the course offerings for the term, she came across one that lit up her face. "Pots," she announced. "I'm going to take pots."

The beginner's pottery course was the perfect blend of creativity and instruction, and she happily brought her projects home to the apartment we shared and displayed them on the windowsill. Vases and bowls predominated. She was learning to work a wheel, so her early efforts were a little lopsided and endearingly flawed (just like the rest of us).

One day, she told me what happened to the real mistakes—the unsalvageable ones. These pitiful scraps, she said, get tossed into a box, only to be soaked in water and broken down until the whole, wet mess can be formed into new clay. The new clay is then given to students to be reformed and reshaped into a vessel worthy of the windowsill in somebody's house.

Jeremiah was commanded to go to the potter's house where he was undoubtedly exposed to the unformed, the malformed, the barely useful, and also, the beautiful pots that lined the potter's windowsills and floor.

Perhaps he had a chance to watch the potter work the clay, stretching and forcing, and shaping it until it was hardly recognizable as the lump it once had been. I can only imagine what effect this had on Jeremiah.

God told Jeremiah that, from before his birth, he was "formed" in the womb, a living model of the being God made from the clay at the beginning of creation. In his life as a prophet, he certainly felt stretched, nearly to the breaking point at times, and forced to do things he would rather not do.

Yet still, he felt compelled to speak the word of God. He said it burned in him and he was he was not always happy about it. At one point he yelled at God, crying out that God had seduced him and he had let himself be seduced. Ultimately, though, he did what God wanted and, in that, found his true form.

By contrast, the inhabitants of Jerusalem resisted the word of God that came from him because it was too demanding. It seemed painful, unpleasant, and unnecessary. Jeremiah's message of destruction for Jerusalem was not taken as a call to change, but rather, as the grumbling of a malcontent. The people took offense.

In our lives, sometimes we are Jeremiah, willing to stretch and grow and be formed, however easy or difficult, and sometimes we are the people of Jerusalem, preferring the easy route and staying away from the potter's hand. Jeremiah's visit to the potter's house at once illuminated his life and the lives of those to whom he preached.

Almost at once we see that the new clay can be coaxed into any shape the artist wants. But as the new clay in God's hands, we also see how God's plans can change when we add our cooperation to the mix. God does not force himself on us. Rather, God offers a relationship, trusting that whatever shape he makes of us will be good enough to grace the windowsills of heaven.

At the same time, we also see how God does not give up on us. However malformed or mistake-riddled we become, God can take us in hand and break us down to start over, forming us into another work of art that shows forth the beauty, delight, and whimsy of the creator. Sometimes, we have to be broken in order to be built up again, but it is comforting to know that even the shattered pieces of our lives can be softened up and remade into clay, that we might have a new shape.

|||||||||||||||||||||||||||||||||

Meditation for Groups or Individuals

When we were children, adventure was defined by risk and proximate danger. "I dare you...I double-dare you," were fighting words. Would we take the dare? Would we do the dangerous thing? Would we tempt fate, or death, or the wrath of parents to sample forbidden fruit?

As we grow older, the risks are of a different kind and the consequences are less sure. Should we take this job or that? Shall we major in math or in music? Is this the person I am supposed to marry or is there another?

All of these answers fall back to us and so, in some sense, are in our control. From that standpoint, we shape our futures and a lot of us like that idea. The parable of the potter confronts us with a different understanding.

The first verse of an old Appalachian hymn by Adelaide A. Pollard goes like this:

"Have thine own way, Lord, have thine own way.
Thou art the Potter, I am the clay.
Mold me and make me after thy will
While I am waiting, yielded and still."

The words dare us to allow God to stretch and shape and form us. They dare us to believe that God does not want to wipe us out, but wants to guide us and give us the grace to be fully who we are and to live into our identities as the image of God. The only way we can do that is to yield, believing that God will not form us into something we are not and that, if we find ourselves ruined by an errant turn on the wheel, or our own wills, God can make the best of us.

Read the passage again and reflect on the following questions:

How hard is it to face starting over when your life flops over on the wheel or collapses inward?

What have been the factors that have shaped and formed you over your life? Where have you been stretched to the breaking point or given a little more to work with? How have you felt God to be present or absent in those times?

How is the hand of God forming you now? When have you stopped still long enough to reflect on that formation and actively cooperated with it?

Imagine simply yielding your life to God and promising nothing else but to do your best with whatever or whoever God has made of you up to this point. What peace or anxiety does that raise in you? Can you imagine that you are good enough to stand on the windowsill of God's house?

*Who or what in your life, besides God, have you allowed to be the
"potter's hands" for good or ill? This might be friends or family,
worry, money, ego, service or anything at all.*

The Prayer of
THE PROPHET WHO GOT A MESSAGE FROM GOD IN AN ART STUDIO

Loving God, Creative God, Maker of all things
    and the One who formed me from the clay of the earth
I so yearn for your touch to make everything right
    and I do not often want to yield to your touch
    which pulls and pushes me
    into a shape I may not want.
Here I stand, not on the Potter's wheel, but next to it
Fascinated by the beauty I see unfolding and building up
    and afraid as I see clay stretched out, folded over,
    worked and reworked
    into a shape worthy of being called the image of its maker.
Could that be me? And can I stand still long enough for you
    to make of me what you will, trusting that it will be
    a thing of beauty…
    trusting that I will be a thing of beauty through your hands.
Even in the asking, your answer comes: "Rest in me," it says.
"Trust in me.:
    for the same care I used at the first, I shall use for you;
    the same love I had for my Child, I will have for you."
Lord, into your hands, I commend my whole being.
Amen.

*What is your prayer to God about being stretched
into different shapes?*

THE PROPHET WHO AUTHENTICATED THE LAW

In the eighteenth year of King Josiah, the king sent Shaphan... to the house of the LORD, saying, "Go up to the high priest Hilkiah, and have him count the entire sum of the money that has been brought into the house of the LORD, which the keepers of the threshold have collected from the people; let it be given into the hand of the workers who have the oversight of the house of the LORD; let them give it to the workers who are at the house of the LORD, repairing the house, that is, to the carpenters, to the builders, to the masons; and let them use it to buy timber and quarried stone to repair the house...." The high priest Hilkiah said to Shaphan the secretary, "I have found the book of the law in the house of the LORD." When Hilkiah gave the book to Shaphan, he read it. Then Shaphan the secretary came to the king, and reported to the king, "Your servants have emptied out the money that was found in the house, and have delivered it into the hand of the workers who have oversight of the house of the LORD." Shaphan the secretary informed the king, "The priest Hilkiah has given me a book." Shaphan then read it aloud to the king.

When the king heard the words of the book of the law, he tore his clothes. Then the king commanded the priest Hilkiah... saying, "Go, inquire of the LORD for me, for the people, and for all Judah, concerning the words of this book that has been found; for great is the wrath of the LORD that is kindled against us, because our ancestors did not obey the words of this book, to do according to all that is written concerning us."

So the priest Hilkiah...went to the prophetess Huldah the wife of Shallum son of Tikvah, son of Harhas, keeper of the wardrobe; she resided in Jerusalem in the Second Quarter, where they consulted her. She declared to them, "Thus says the LORD, the God of Israel: Tell the man who sent you to me, Thus says the LORD, I will indeed bring disaster on this place and on its inhabitants—all the words of the book that the king of Judah has read. Because they have abandoned me and have made offerings to other gods, so that they have provoked me to anger with all the work of their hands, therefore my wrath will be kindled against this place, and it will not be quenched. But as to the king of Judah, who sent you to inquire of the LORD, thus shall you say to him, Thus says the LORD, the God of Israel: Regarding the words that you have heard, because your heart was penitent, and you humbled yourself before the LORD, when you heard how I spoke against this place, and against its inhabitants, that they should become a desolation and a curse, and because you have torn your clothes and wept before me, I also have heard you, says the LORD. Therefore, I will gather you to your ancestors, and you shall be gathered to your grave in peace; your eyes shall not see all the disaster that I will bring on this place." They took the message back to the king.

II KINGS 22:3–20

‖‖‖‖‖‖‖‖‖‖‖‖‖‖‖‖‖‖‖‖‖‖‖‖‖‖‖‖

The Backstory

After the reign of Solomon, the son of David, Israel was divided into two kingdoms, the northern kingdom of Israel and the southern kingdom of Judah. The story of those kingdoms is told in the two books of Kings through the lens of the historian we call the Deuteronomist. His narration was designed to warn the people of Israel about the consequences of disobedience to God.

If we were to read the books of Kings from beginning to end, we would find that the kings of the time were judged by how well they followed in the footsteps of their ancestor David in being obedient to the law of God. Most of the kings failed miserably, but two were very good in the eyes of the Deuteronomist. Those two were Hezekiah and Josiah, both kings of Judah.

It is also in the books of Kings that the prophets begin to make their mark as "troublers" of Israel. The court prophets like Nathan in I Kings serve as advisors to the king and call him to account for his sins. But, prophets like Elijah and Elisha are not connected to the courts. Rather, they traveled the countryside and regularly challenged the kings to turn away from their rebellion and return to the Lord. Huldah, one of the few biblical women named in the profession (Deborah is another), seems to belong to the group of prophets who were connected to one location and had the gift of discerning the will of God. The Israelites were accustomed to come to them regularly for judgment or consultation on important matters of the day.

This story of Huldah takes place in 622 BC, when Josiah saw the neglect of the temple and ordered carpenters and masons to repair its walls. (Jeremiah did some of his preaching during this time as well.)

During the reconstruction, he uncovered a book of the Law that many scholars believe to be Deuteronomy 5 and 12–26. When Shaphan, a scribe, read the words of the Law to the king, the king immediately tore his clothes (a sign of great sorrow and repentance) because he recognized the extent of the people's disobedience.

It was important, however, to have the book authenticated, thus Josiah sent it to the prophet Huldah. She delivers a message of destruction for Jerusalem, but tells Josiah that his goodness and repentance will allow him to live out his days in peace, and he will not see the devastation to come.

Her prophecy comes true. Josiah dies defending Jerusalem from Neco, king of Egypt. The southern kingdom of Judah finally ends for good when King Nebuchadnazzar of Babylon invades and destroys the capital city of Jerusalem in 587 BC. (The northern kingdom of Israel fell to Assyria a century before Josiah ordered repairs to the temple.) The Deuteronomist tells us that no king before or after Josiah turned to the Lord "with all his heart and with all his soul and with all his might" (words that echo the first of Jewish and Christian laws about how we are to love God).

As for Huldah, the six verses that refer to her in the entire story (and their counterparts in 2 Chronicles 34:23–28) are the only traces of her life that we have. She remains nearly forgotten, but without her, Josiah might not have recognized the importance of what he had found or what it meant to Judah.

||||||||||||||||||||||||||||||

What Does This Story Tell Us?

Huldah, a prophet, a wife, and an inhabitant of Jerusalem shows up only once in the Hebrew Bible. We do not hear about her before Josiah sends her the book of the Law which was found in the temple, nor will we hear about her after her message is delivered.

When the prophets are named in classrooms or trivia games, she will rarely, if ever, be among them. She lives her life in the same relative obscurity as most of us, unknown except to family and friends and the local inhabitants, unless or until some unexpected event lifts us into the limelight briefly.

What we have to remember, though, is that those moments when we step out (or are brought out) of our comfort zones are possible only because of the many moments we have put into doing what we do every day.

Huldah practiced her ministry of prophecy long enough that she built up a local reputation. People knew her by name and where she lived and that she was reliable in her understanding and interpretation of God's word.

They also knew she would not flinch at the hard messages, nor ignore the easier ones. She had earned the trust of others in small matters and when the time came for the important task of authenticating the law, Josiah trusted her again. (Centuries later, Jesus, in one of his parables, would say that those who could be trusted in small matters would be trusted with even greater things—see Matthew 25:14–30.)

Huldah used the gifts that God had given her every day and so was ready when God most needed to work through her. The first lesson that Huldah teaches us is that we must do what is put before us with integrity and faithfulness, for the glory of God. That is our call and our challenge.

The second lesson we learn comes from looking at the message Huldah sent back to the king. It was not a hopeful one. In her one fleeting moment of fame, she had to deliver a prophecy of the destruction of Jerusalem.

Sometimes our service to God includes the realization that God's desire for us is often thwarted by human freedom. Not even the good news of God's presence saves every person who hears it.

The inhabitants of Jerusalem were unconcerned about their own destructive behavior. They followed their own desires; God allowed them to do so, and Babylon became the instrument of their destruction. I am not sure that Huldah would have wanted to give that message, but her ministry compelled her to truthfulness.

Huldah was also able to interpret God's care for those who turned toward him. She told Josiah that his repentance was more than acceptable and he would finish his life before the Babylonians destroyed the city.

We cannot always do whatever we want with our gifts. We cannot always have the easy path. Sometimes we have to do what is hard or what is disturbing. Huldah knew that. Following her example, we, too, can do what needs to be done, confident that God stands with us even, or especially, in the difficult moments.

||||||||||||||||||||||||||||||

Meditation for Groups or Individuals

What is it that we have been given to do and how do we use our gifts to do it well? These two questions are at the core of our lives.

In every stage we wonder if we are making a difference in the world or even just in the lives of those we touch. We think about the gifts we have (or that others have told us we have) and ask whether or not we are using them as best we can.

The questions become acute when we have to say or do the unpopular thing or when we are confronted with delivering unpopular messages for the good of others. It is not any easier when the voice inside of us tells us what we do not want to hear—that we have been wrong or we need to change.

If we have experienced any of these moments, we have had a little glimpse of what Huldah's job entailed. We have been prophets in our own day-to-day living.

So what are the gifts that parents, teachers, friends, pastors, bosses, or siblings need to be "prophetic" about, and call those under their care (and themselves) to faithfulness and to a better way of life?

Certainly, we need the graces of patience and love to correct the behavior of a child or call a friend to account for actions taken. The example of Huldah also tells something else: there must be some measure of consistency in our daily actions—people need to know they can count on our presence and faithfulness to what we see and hear.

Those who have had the challenge of deciding that an employee was not a good fit or that he or she was being put on probation need compassion and empathy coupled with firmness and resolve. And all of us need the grace of humor and the fullness of humility to know that we are not always right and need correction from time to time.

These same gifts help us on the other side as well, when as bosses, parents, and friends, we must deal with whatever crisis that rocks our foundations. When the World Trade Center fell, the CEO of one company took the responsibility to call the families of his employees killed in the attack. He did it from a pay phone in Canada because all the flights were grounded and his cell phone was not working. I think he felt compelled by compassion and love to walk with these families even or especially when the devastating news came to them.

We are not all famous or well-known. But consistent, quiet, prophetic leadership—like Huldah's—done in the towns, schools, homes, and workplaces of our lives gives God the opportunity to draw on a rich harvest of people who might be asked to do even greater things when the time comes.

Read the story of Huldah again and reflect on the following questions:

Do you know what your gifts are at home, at work, or at school? What are they, and how do you practice using them?

How hard is it for you to say or do the unpopular thing, even if you know it's right? What do you ask of God in those instances?

Have there been any times and places in which you had to tell someone bad news? How did you handle it? Which of your gifts did you use to do that?

Are there any places in your life where you are the "authority" or leader that someone (or everyone) else relies on? What are the challenges that are implicit in that? What gifts do you use most frequently when you are called to act as that authority? Do some feel more natural than others?

Have you ever had to do something extremely important? If so, what happened and how did you feel both about leaving your comfort zone, and then returning to it?

If someone were to seek you at "the place where you resided," where would find you most at home? Where and with whom are you fully yourself?

The Prayer of
THE PROPHET WHO AUTHENTICATED THE LAW

Dear Lord,
What is it you are asking me to do now?
I have been content to live out my life with the little things
   you have given me to do.
They have been hard enough work, but still I have had time
   for rest and taking my delight in those around me
I have felt useful and well-used by your will, glad to be of service
   and proud to be called by name.
But now, you have given me something else that
   makes me reach beyond myself
Your voice has come front and center and your words
   are so important I worry that I will not get them right.
I can only do my best and offer it to you
   It will not be easy, and for some it will not be welcome.
But still you call my name, and name your gifts in me,
   and reveal your word
   and still I know I will answer.
And when this work—your work—is finished,
   I will return to my quiet life
   to live out my days in service, unremarkable, but faithful
with your voice in the background, quietly urging me on.
Blessed by the Lord who has given me all good things.
Amen.

*What is your prayer to God about the gifts you have been given
and the "prophetic" leadership you sometimes have to take on?*

THE PROPHET WHO CHOSE A KING (TWICE)

The LORD said to Samuel, "How long will you grieve over Saul? I have rejected him from being king over Israel. Fill your horn with oil and set out; I will send you to Jesse the Bethlehemite, for I have provided for myself a king among his sons." Samuel did what the LORD commanded, and came to Bethlehem. The elders of the city came to meet him trembling, and said, "Do you come peaceably?" He said, "Peaceably; I have come to sacrifice to the LORD; sanctify yourselves and come with me to the sacrifice." And he sanctified Jesse and his sons and invited them to the sacrifice.

When they came, he looked on Eliab and thought, "Surely the LORD's anointed is now before the LORD." But the LORD said to Samuel, "Do not look on his appearance or on the height of his stature, because I have rejected him; for the LORD does not see as mortals see; they look on the outward appearance, but the LORD looks on the heart." Then Jesse called Abinadab, and made him pass before Samuel. He said, "Neither has the LORD chosen this one." Then Jesse made Shammah pass by. And he said, "Neither has the LORD chosen this one." Jesse made seven of his sons pass before Samuel, and Samuel said to Jesse, "The LORD has not chosen any of these." Samuel said to Jesse, "Are all your sons here?" And he said, "There remains yet the youngest, but he is keeping the sheep." And Samuel said to Jesse, "Send and bring him; for we will not sit down until he comes here." He sent and brought him in. Now he was ruddy, and had beautiful eyes, and was handsome. The LORD said, "Rise and anoint him; for this is the one." Then Samuel took the horn of oil, and anointed him in the presence of his brothers; and the spirit of the LORD came mightily upon David from that day forward. Samuel then set out and went to Ramah.

I SAMUEL 16:1, 4–13

||||||||||||||||||||||||||||||||||||

The Backstory

Samuel occupies a unique place among Israel's great characters. He is the bridge between the period of the Judges and the era of the prophets. His birth to a barren woman named Hannah, who prays to God for a child, is clearly presented as divine intervention. And, if biblical stories have taught us anything, it is that when God enters into human history, nothing will ever be the same again.

Hannah's prayer at the birth of her son is one of joyful surprise at God's actions throughout the world and has many similarities to the *Magnificat* that Mary speaks when she visits Elizabeth (Luke 1:46–55).

As a young boy, Samuel receives messages from God and is later acknowledged as a prophet. In the absence of a king, however, Samuel also serves as a leader of the people, much like the judges before him.

In the first book of Samuel, we read the story of his birth, his commitment to serve the Lord, and the anointing of not one, but two kings in spite of some serious reservations about the process.

The first person he anoints as king is Saul, who might have done a decent job had he not taken matters into his own hands during a battle, disobeying the commands of God which Samuel had given him.

The consequences for Saul were devastating. We are told that God "regrets" that he made Saul king. In reality, the word that is used is closer in meaning to "repent" or "change one's mind." In either case, Samuel grieved over the loss of this king he had anointed.

The two books of Samuel join the two books of Kings in telling the history of Israel during the monarchy. In the Jewish Bible these books are part of the "former prophets" because the story itself serves to challenge people to return to the law and be faithful to God. Prophets were the people chosen to carry that message of God to the people.

############################

What Does This Story Tell Us?

For many of us in our day-to-day living, nothing is more disturbing than the unexpected surprise that overthrows our plans and forces a change in direction. Have you ever experienced the sudden illness of a child before a big presentation at work, a computer crash when a project is due, a car's empty gas gauge as you hurry to an appointment? How about the unforeseen bill that disrupts the budget? All of these (and many more) make life more challenging and less comfortable. They remind us that we are not in control and that, many times, we are just playing catch-up with the little details of our lives.

But we also know that the best-laid plans are not foolproof. In the beginning of this story, even God's plan to have Saul as king doesn't work out, but falls victim to Saul's free will and very human weakness in the face of temptation. (During the year when the Chicago White Sox won the World Series, someone asked Cardinal George, Archbishop of Chicago, if the White Sox would win. With good humor, he replied, "It's God's will that the White Sox win the pennant… Of course, God's will is often thwarted by human freedom." It was a masterful way to account for either outcome.) But Samuel grieves over the failure of God's plan as though it were his own.

Perhaps he felt complicit in it; perhaps he thought, "If God can't get it right, what chance do any of us have?" Maybe he wondered whether the people of Israel were ready for God's plans at all. In any case, the king he anointed at God's request failed to follow the Lord's command.

Still, whatever the reason for his distress, Samuel demonstrates at least two things we would do well to follow when our plans suddenly change. Samuel hears the voice of God in his grieving, and he listens to it. That bears repeating. Samuel hears God *in his grieving* about plans gone awry.

Now, what he hears surely took him a minute to comprehend.

God tells him to go and anoint someone else—to go and do the same thing he had done before.

I imagine Samuel standing, open-mouthed, at this command. What guarantee does he have that it would not go badly again? The answer is "none." God gives no guarantee that anything we do, or participate in, will turn out the way we think it should or even the way God thinks it should. God promises only to be with us and to make the best of whatever comes, good or bad, regardless of the most carefully laid-out plans.

Samuel's second lesson for us unfolds in the main part of the story. God reveals divine plans to a heart that is open and does not assume that we know better than God.

Samuel thought he knew exactly the kind of person God would pick for king—someone older, wiser, and more mature. In Samuel's mind, an eldest son would certainly be the most viable candidate.

God's pick confounded his expectations. The youngest son, the shepherd, would be anointed king at God's command. Samuel had to trust what he was hearing and had to trust that God sees rightly.

So often our own expectations get in the way both of our decision-making and of God's plans. Trusting God to tell us the truth in whatever change of plans or direction we might experience is the hardest task of all.

Also in this story, God displays two traits for which he is known in the Old Testament. God lets us go if that is what we want, free to follow our own desires even if they are not good. When we read that God regrets or repents, it is not because God is capricious. Rather, God realizes that some people are not ready for a close relationship with him.

Of course God also allows anyone and everyone to turn toward him and confounds our expectations in the other direction. Another prophet, Jonah, preached the destruction of Ninevah. When the Ninevites repented of their wickedness, God decided not to destroy them, leaving Jonah angry that what he had prophesied had not come true.

Samuel's story also shows us that God does not give up. Rather, God calls to us in our grief over the loss of our plans. He calls to us when we doubt that things can work out at all and tells us it is time to get moving. There are other plans to be carried out and new directions to explore. This is not always easy for us to hear or to do. Sometimes God's plans don't look like much at first. We think we know a better way. But consider this: God's persistence, together with our cooperation, can do more than we ever thought possible.

Meditation for Groups or Individuals

The great prayer of St. Ignatius, the *Suscipe*, begins like this: "Take, Lord, receive all my liberty…" The prayer offers everything we have, think, or desire to God and asks for nothing but God's love and grace. At heart, it is a prayer about flexibility and allowing God to place in our hands whatever God deems necessary for us. And it is a prayer about giving up trying to control everything (or everyone) in our lives.

But learning to be flexible and learning to let go of control are both tough nuts to crack. We like to know what is happening, or at least the possibilities. We want to plan our lives to some extent. We may understand that there are more ways of doing things, but don't we often think we know the one best way?

And many of us are not good at change, be it sudden or gradual. The things in our lives that send us into a tailspin are those that take control from us, placing our dependence on God and others for direction and peace. About two-thirds of the psalms deal with plans gone awry as the cries of, "How long, O Lord," or, "Hear my voice, O God, in my complaint," echo out into the darkness.

Samuel faced two moments when his assumptions about unfolding plans were called into question. The first was when the king whom he anointed failed to comply with God's will, preferring instead to follow his own path. No doubt Samuel wondered whether he or God had failed.

God simply acknowledged Samuel's grief, reminded him who was in charge, and told him there was still work to be done. When Samuel faced ten of Jesse's sons, any of whom could be king, he heard the voice of God telling him not to look at appearances, or at his own expectations or assumptions, but to trust that God knew the heart and would unfold his desire when the time came.

Samuel received two graces from God in that moment. One was the ability to be flexible in the face of instability, and the other was the ability to let go of the need to control destiny. Samuel, by laying the future in God's hands, found a king to rule Israel. Perhaps with a little flexibility and our own understanding about who's in charge, we might find our own path in God's plans.

Read the story of Samuel again and reflect on these questions:

Have things in your life gone pretty much as you planned or have there been a few detours along the way where you felt you did not know what was coming next? If so, what have those been and how did you deal with them?

When you got back on the road, how were things the same or different? Were you even headed in the same direction?

Did God seem present or absent to you in those moments? Was there ever a point in which you wanted to say, "Come on, God, you have got to be kidding!"

In the grief that comes in profound moments of change, how has God invited you to return to your life and to the particular journey you are on?

Where are the areas in which you want real control in your life? Can you imagine giving those areas over to God and saying with all your heart, "Lord, I know you never give up; I will accept from you whatever happens here."

The Prayer of
THE PROPHET WHO CHOSE A KING (TWICE)

I am not sure what I am doing, Lord,
 I know only that you want me to do it
 and I cannot see what will come of your wanting it.
For my whole life you have called my name
 in the dark of night and in the dark of life
 and I have tried to respond as I did at the first:
"Lord, speak, for your servant is listening."
But it did not always work out as I had hoped or, perhaps,
 as you had hoped either.
 and I have sometimes grown weary from hoping so much
 and sometimes getting so little from working so hard,
 only to have the unexpected keep me from the rewards
 I thought I wanted.
And then you come again, calling my name,
 wanting me in your service
 commanding me to try again and let you be the one in charge.
Well, here I am—again—and I will try to let you be in charge
 and know that the work worth doing is the work you give me,
 the service worth taking on is the service in your name
 and the hope that endures is the hope that I will
 see you face to face
 with all those whom you call to your love.
Amen.

*How would you talk with God about the way things have worked
out in your life and how you have felt (or not felt) the presence of
God in that?*

KINGS

In the beginning, Israel had no king. The Lord was ruler over all, and the people of Israel were God's people. To be sure, there were leaders in Moses and the judges that followed in his wake, but somewhere between 1200 and 1000 BC, the people began to look for a leader who was more like what they saw in their Near Eastern counterparts.

Predictably, some factions thought that having a king meant that Israel no longer thought of God as its ruler; others thought a strong leader would help Israel negotiate relationships with other nations. Ultimately Israel decided to have a king, looking to God for a sign about who it should be.

When the Deuteronomist, the historian/theologian, looked back on that period, he reflected on the place of the king among God's people and wrote about it in a way that left little doubt regarding who ruled. The book of Deuteronomy tells us that the sole job of the king of Israel was not to lead armies or make laws.

Rather, Deuteronomy says, "...he shall have a copy of this law made from the scroll that is in the custody of the Levitical priests. He shall keep it with him and read it all the days of his life that he may learn to fear the Lord, his God, and to heed and fulfill all the words of this law and these statutes." (Deuteronomy 17:18–19)

The king's job, his life's mission, if you will, was to be an example of what it means to be obedient to God.

Read in that light, we understand why the inscription above Jesus' cross was so ironic. Pilate thought he was insulting Jesus and all the Jews by crucifying the "king of the Jews" as a common criminal. Instead, he was drawing attention to the nature of kingship that was not of this world. Jesus was king of the Jews *par excellence* because he was obedient to God even to death on the cross.

Imagine what might happen if all the leaders in the world read the great love commandments every day and took to heart the idea that they had to be an example of this love: "You shall love the Lord, your God, with all your heart and all your mind and all your strength, and you shall love your neighbor as yourself."

What do you think would happen?

Two of the kings we meet in these stories are kings of Israel, and both have their moments of great obedience as well as their moments of great human failure.

The third king is a king of Egypt who is visited by God in his sleep and is compelled to obey him. Sometimes, even those who do not believe as we do, or perhaps do not believe at all, can hear the word of God, know it for what it is, and teach others to obey it.

THE KING WHO TRUSTED IN GOD

In the fourteenth year of King Hezekiah, Sennacherib, king of Assyria, went on an expedition against all the fortified cities of Judah and captured them…The king of Assyria sent the general, the lord chamberlain, and the commander from Lachish with a great army to King Hezekiah at Jerusalem…They called for the king, who sent out to them Eliakim…the master of the palace, Shebnah, the scribe, and the herald Joah…The commander said to them, "Tell Hezekiah, 'thus says the great king of Assyria: On what do you base this confidence of yours? Do you think mere words substitute for strategy and might in war? On whom, then do you rely, that you rebel against me? This Egypt, the staff on which you rely, is in fact a broken reed which pierces the hand of anyone who leans on it. That is what Pharaoh, king of Egypt, is to all who rely on him…' "

The commander returned, and found the king of Assyria fighting against Libnah; for he had heard that the king had left Lachish…The king of Assyria heard a report that the king of Ethiopia had come out to fight against him. Again he sent messengers to Hezekiah, saying, "Thus shall you speak to King Hezekiah of Judah: Do not let your God on whom you rely deceive you by promising that Jerusalem will not be given into the hand of the king of Assyria. See, you have heard what the kings of Assyria have done to all lands, destroying them utterly. Shall you be delivered? Have the gods of the nations delivered them, the nations that my predecessors destroyed, Gozan, Haran, Rezeph, and the people of Eden who were in Telassar? Where is the king of Hamath, the king of Arpad, the king of the city of Sepharvaim, the king of Hena, or the king of Ivvah?"

Hezekiah received the letter from the hand of the messengers and read it; then Hezekiah went up to the house of the LORD and spread it before the LORD. And Hezekiah prayed before the LORD, and said: "O LORD the God of Israel, who are enthroned above the cherubim, you are God, you alone, of all the kingdoms of the earth; you have made heaven and earth. Incline your ear, O LORD, and hear; open your eyes, O LORD, and see; hear the words of Sennacherib, which he has sent to mock the living God. Truly, O LORD, the kings of Assyria have laid waste the nations and their lands, and have hurled their gods into the fire, though they were no gods but the work of human hands—wood and stone—and so they were destroyed. So now, O LORD our God, save us, I pray you, from his hand, so that all the kingdoms of the earth may know that you, O LORD, are God alone."

II KINGS 18:13,17–21 (NAB); 19:8–19 (NRSV)

||||||||||||||||||||||||||||||||||

The Backstory

King Hezekiah was one of the very good kings in the history of Israel, as stated in the second book of Kings. As such, he stood out among so many others who were disobedient and rebellious toward God. His behavior during the Assyrian crisis (745–640 BC) cemented his legacy as the king who refused to abandon God (unlike his predecessor Ahaz).

The kingdom of Israel was divided into two after the reign of Solomon. Among the great world powers of the time, Egypt was in the foreground, but Assyria was gaining in force and finally invaded the northern kingdom (named Israel) and its capital, Samaria, an account of which can be found just before our story in II Kings 18:9–12.

Scripture records the reason for the attack this way: "…because they did not obey the voice of the LORD their God but transgressed his covenant—all that Moses the servant of the LORD had commanded; they neither listened nor obeyed." It was both an indictment of them, and a warning to future generations not to fall in the same path.

A few years later, when the king of Assyria captured the fortified cities of the southern kingdom of Judah, Hezekiah, who was king of Judah, paid him a tribute in the hope that the kingdom would be left alone.

In return, Sennacherib, king of Assyria, bullied him. "Your faith is no match for horses and war strategies," he told him. "Egypt, on whom you rely, can never stand against us."

The servants of Sennacherib even went so far as to tempt Hezekiah's servants and the people of Jerusalem, offering them horses and riches. They told them not to let Hezekiah deceive them because he would never be able to deliver them from Assyria's power.

Another king might have run to Egypt or another nation, begging for help against Assyria. Hezekiah refused to do so. Instead, he prayed to God and God answered his prayer.

What Does This Story Tell Us?

"I want to do it myself," is a child's cry. Even when we get older, the desire to discover new things on our own, to figure out how to solve problems when they arise, and to find our own resources to make our way is a strong impulse.

When a bully taunts us, we hide in humiliation, but resolve to become stronger. Hezekiah's kingship was characterized by his trust in God, his obedience to the commandments of God, and his destruction of idols and worship sites. Sennacherib, though, tested his resolve.

Hezekiah could have been like every other king in the area, forging alliances, and amassing great armies. He might have relied on strategies that ensured victory or trained spies to seek out weaknesses. But that was not the king's place as Hezekiah saw it.

Hezekiah was so strong in his trust that he trained his servants and those people who were at the wall of Jerusalem to ignore taunts of Sennacherib's emissaries.

When Sennacherib questioned the power of the Lord and told Hezekiah that God could not help Jerusalem escape its fate, Hezekiah did what early practice and adult faith demanded. He placed everything into the hands of God and trusted in God's power, rather than in armies or deception. For this king, there was only one ruler and that was the Lord.

Sennacherib's mocking derision presented a real temptation for Hezekiah. Facing certain destruction, almost anyone would try to prove they could overcome trouble themselves.

But Sennacherib, showing him the ruins of other nations whose gods did not protect them, was also tempting Hezekiah not to believe in God as a savior. In order to trust in God, Hezekiah had to let go of any need to prove that he was a great king (at least according to the world's standard of kingship) and to reaffirm his identity as a servant of God.

His prayer tells us much of what we need to know about him. The first sentence gives us the lens through which Hezekiah sees. This is the "God of Israel" who is personally involved with his people, the One to whom Israel can turn.

This is God who is higher than any other, "enthroned above the cherubim." This is God who alone is king of all the kingdoms of the earth and the one who made heaven and earth.

God's relationship does not stop with Israel, but extends to all of creation. In naming all the kingdoms of the earth, Hezekiah humbles himself, recognizing that the title of king fades before God's authority.

Finally, Hezekiah asks that God see and hear what Sennacherib is doing, pointing out that Sennacherib has destroyed the gods of all the other nations. Hezekiah trusts that the Lord of all will not suffer the same fate.

At the very end, he appeals: "...Save us, I pray you from his hand, so that all the kingdoms of earth may know that you, O LORD, are God alone." Hidden in that phrase, though, is Hezekiah's concern that Sennacherib will believe himself to be God in true megalomaniac fashion. But Hezekiah's hope and his faith assure him that God can stop that from happening.

Two things stand out about Hezekiah.

The first is his refusal to succumb to the bully who taunts him and the temptation to rely on himself and/or others to achieve all his desires.

The second is his faith that recognizes God as Lord of all and his immediate, heartfelt prayer, asking what seems to be impossible.

Because he knows God in the personal relationship with the Israelites as his people and with the world as the Creator, he will see God's presence in whatever comes of this prayer request, even if it does not turn out exactly as he would like.

We, too, know God in personal relationship with each one of us and with the community of faith. We confess God as the creator of the world, and we can bring our heart's desires to him, knowing that God will be with us in whatever comes.

By the way, God does answer Hezekiah's prayer: "Therefore thus says the LORD concerning the king of Assyria: He shall not come into this city, shoot an arrow there, come before it with a shield, or cast up a siege-ramp against it. By the way that he came, by the same he shall return; he shall not come into this city, says the LORD. For I will defend this city to save it, for my own sake and for the sake of my servant David." (II Kings 19:32–34)

||||||||||||||||||||||||||||||||

Meditation for Groups or Individuals

Trust in God comes easily when things are going well. Good times bolster our confidence that we are doing the right thing and everything is going as planned.

During more chaotic times, trust comes a little harder. Chaos might be internal or external, personal or communal, coming from human will or borne of natural disasters. Whatever the source, chaos disrupts our confidence, questions our judgment, and leaves us seeking a solution.

And every now and then, we are tempted. "If you were really good you could find a way out...If you are so smart then why is your life in trouble...If God loved you, God would not have let this happen." In other words, we are tempted to believe a lie: that we are no good, that we are not smart, and that God does not love and care for us.

Such catastrophes, big or small, might have us looking for any way out. The number of self-help books on the shelves at the local bookstore and the pleas for financial aid that flood our inboxes and mailboxes suggest that we use our own resources to help find a solution, and certainly we have many from which to draw—our own intelligence, the gifts God has given us, and friends and family whose strength and love can help us through the worst of times (and are gifts of God in a different way).

"God helps those who help themselves," we say and we set about to do just that, forgetting sometimes that we will not always have the control we want and that we are not always able to see the best solution to the issues at hand.

While Hezekiah did not have self-help books, he certainly had advisors and friends, and he used them when it was appropriate. But Hezekiah also refused to believe the lie that God was incapable of helping him.

This is the other side of our self reliance: "Let go and let God," we remind ourselves when we try too hard to insert ourselves and our wills into hurtful situations. Here Hezekiah is a model: he had practiced prayer and obedience to God throughout his life, even in the good times, so when the chaos of Sennacherib's invasion came, he did not hesitate to come to God again.

Were Sennacherib to come to us today, perhaps his taunts would be a little different: "Where are your rulers and your presidents whom you hold so dear? If your God were truly God, why did he allow so much destruction in this flood or that attack? Do you think anyone in the world will help you now? They are all too busy."

After doing the best we can, we might follow Hezekiah, who showed us what it means to place our trust in God and live through chaotic times. He believed that God would never abandon Israel.

In later centuries, Jesus told us that God the Father will not leave us orphans in this world. And in our own lives, there have been too many instances of a sudden light in a dark time, heralded by the out-pouring of help from total strangers, or the love of family and friends.

There has even been someone who was willing to die so that we might live. God does not always intervene directly nor in the time frame we would like, but God can and has come in the most unexpected of disguises and with just what we need at the time.

Read the passage again and reflect on the following questions:

How do you pray and show your trust in God when times are good?

Think of a time of personal chaos. Were you tempted to give up on God altogether and do things yourself? Who or what tempted you most? In what ways? What happened to your prayer and trust in God during that time?

Can you look back on some events in your life and say, "The hand of God was there, but I did not know it at the time?" What happened in those events?

The Prayer of
THE KING WHO TRUSTED IN GOD

Lord of all, in heaven and on earth
I know you in my life and in the lives of my ancestors.
I know you have not abandoned them
    and I trust that you will not abandon me.
Sometimes when I look at the world now
    I see so many things begging for my allegiance
    trying to prove to me that you are no longer worthy
    of my trust or my love
        showing me the many places where they say
        you have failed
And, yet, and yet—my heart knows what happens
    when your grace and human will come together for good.
My soul rejoices when your Spirit
    rushes in with wind-blown force and makes itself known
    in the cry of the poor and their teaching
    and in the compassion of those who open
    hearts and minds to them,
        learning as they use your gifts for all.
My own spirit lifts up when prayer and sacrament and
    the companionship of faith
        make your presence known to me and give me
        the strength to go forth.
Help me trust in you now; even in the dark
    when I do not understand
        for your dark is not dark at all.
You are my light and my salvation.
Amen.

What is your prayer of trust to God?

THE KING WHO DREAMED ABOUT AN UNKNOWN GOD

From there Abraham journeyed toward the region of the Negeb, and settled between Kadesh and Shur. While residing in Gerar as an alien, Abraham said of his wife, Sarah, "She is my sister." And King Abimelech of Gerar sent and took Sarah.

But God came to Abimelech in a dream by night, and said to him, "You are about to die because of the woman whom you have taken; for she is a married woman." Now Abimelech had not approached her; so he said, "LORD, will you destroy an innocent people? Did he not himself say to me, 'She is my sister'? And she herself said, 'He is my brother.' I did this in the integrity of my heart and the innocence of my hands." Then God said to him in the dream, "Yes, I know that you did this in the integrity of your heart; furthermore it was I who kept you from sinning against me. Therefore I did not let you touch her. Now then, return the man's wife; for he is a prophet, and he will pray for you and you shall live. But if you do not restore her, know that you shall surely die, you and all that are yours."

So Abimelech rose early in the morning, and called all his servants and told them all these things; and the men were very much afraid. Then Abimelech called Abraham, and said to him, "What have you done to us? How have I sinned against you, that you have brought such great guilt on me and my kingdom? You have done things to me that ought not to be done." And Abimelech said to Abraham, "What were you thinking of, that you did this thing?" Abraham said, "I did it because I thought, There is no fear of God at all in this place, and they will kill me because of my wife. Besides, she is indeed my sister, the daughter of my father but not the daughter of my mother; and she became my wife. And when God caused me to wander from my father's house, I said to her, 'This is the kindness you must do me: at every place to which we come, say of me, He is my brother.'"

Then Abimelech took sheep and oxen, and male and female slaves, and gave them to Abraham, and restored his wife, Sarah, to him. Abimelech said, "My land is before you; settle where it pleases you." To Sarah he said, "Look, I have given your brother a thousand pieces of silver; it is your exoneration before all who are with you; you are completely vindicated." Then Abraham prayed to God; and God healed Abimelech, and also healed his wife and female slaves so that they bore children. For the LORD had closed fast all the wombs of the house of Abimelech because of Sarah, Abraham's wife.

GENESIS 20:1–18

||||||||||||||||||||||||||||||

The Backstory

This story of Abraham, Sarah, and Abimelech, king of Gerar, is the second of three similar narratives in Genesis. The first also records that Abraham passed Sarah off as his sister to Pharaoh, king of Egypt, for fear that he would be killed (Genesis 12:1–20).

The third is a story about Abraham's son, Isaac, his wife, Rebecca, and Abimelech, king of the Philistines at Gerar. Most scholars are convinced that these are all versions of the same story, told from different traditions.

Our story is from a tradition that many call the *Elohist*, in part because the Hebrew word for God in this story is *Elohim*. We also know from other passages that the Elohist does not like the idea of God speaking with human beings face-to-face. Rather, his stories emphasize a "one-step removed" policy and God speaks in visions and dreams.

Even if this is one of three versions of a story, we should note that repetition often draws attention to characters and situations that might otherwise go unnoticed.

When we come into this story, Sarah has already laughed at the word of a complete stranger who has promised that she will have a child.

Abraham has argued with God over the proposed destruction of Sodom and Gomorrah, asking that God not destroy the city if even ten good people could be found.

And Lot, Abraham's nephew, has fled from Sodom and Gomorrah with his wife and two of his daughters. His wife did not make it to safety, but he managed to climb into the hills with his daughters, each of whom became the mother to a nation.

Of Abimelech, we know nothing until he appears in our story as king of Gerar, near the Mediterranean Sea, southwest of the land of Canaan between Gaza and Beer-Sheba.

As a king, he was accustomed to taking whomever he wanted into his house as a servant or wife. It was the king's privilege for allowing the people into his land. The story of Abimelech's near encounter with disaster, among other things, assures us that Isaac is truly the son of Abraham and that God is truly the Ruler of the world.

What Does This Story Tell Us?

When we read this story today, do we feel a little uncomfortable at the depiction of God? Does God really threaten to punish people who do things they have no idea are wrong? Can't we expect a learning curve and more than one chance to get things right?

Part of what we see in this story is the theological understanding that God's law is universal and obedience to God is necessary for life. We also see that God does give chances to those who stumble in ignorance, even if those chances come in some surprising and momentarily unnerving ways.

Abimelech (the name means "the king is my father") could not have known the God who had made a covenant with Abraham and promised him a son. How then could he not only recognize this voice out of his deep sleep but also argue with it about the finer points of guilt and innocence? There can be only one answer: when God decides to intervene in human affairs, his voice and will are profoundly compelling.

Perhaps we envy the clarity with which God speaks to Abimelech: "This is what is wrong; this is how you will handle it; this is what will happen if you don't." God leaves no room for error, nor does he leave any doubt.

Abimelech wakes up and immediately does as the Lord asks. While we might have laughed a little at this story of deception, we might also have said to ourselves: "If only the voice of God was that clear to me."

On a deeper level, though, the story of Abimelech shows us two things about God.

First, God will speak to whoever needs it, whenever God chooses, and by whatever means God has at his disposal.

For Abimelech it was in a dream; for us it might be through a friend, in the words of a book, or in the awe of natural beauty or nature's power. For those tempted to think that God speaks only to the privileged or the chosen, this might be discomforting as well.

Abimelech was a foreign king, so why should God care whether he lived or died? The truth is, God's care is not bound by neighborhood lines, borders of countries, or religious denominations. Nor is God constrained by any sense we might have of privilege, place, or the assurance that comes from a people who think they know God.

God, in his own way, chose to warn Abimelech of his transgression and gave him a chance to correct it.

Second, God's word comes to us whenever we are most open to it. That is why some of the best conversations and the best prayers happen at night when our defenses are down. God's word might interrupt our lives at any point because God wants us to do right and good, even when we think we have been doing that all along.

Of course, it would be a mistake to say that God only speaks to us when we are in trouble; God's message of a son for Abraham and Sarah shows otherwise. It strikes me, though, that the voice of the well-formed conscience serves as a conduit for God's concern when we do something that is less than honorable. Abimelech may have known something about that.

Abimelech teaches us something about ourselves as well. If we live our lives with integrity and care, we can stand before God, trusting that he guards our going and our coming even when we do things that are wrong and do not know it.

When we try to do right and live lives that earnestly seek God, we shall surely find him—or he will find us—and we will know him.

Abimelech, the foreign king, engages God in conversation. He listens, talks, and even disagrees; but, ultimately, he believes what his heart is telling him is true: This is the Lord of the entire world. Abimelech obeys the Lord who cost him his sleep and, in the process, becomes an example of obedience.

iiiiiiiiiiiiiiiiiiiiiiiiiiiiiiiii

Meditation for Groups or Individuals

We cannot know when the voice of God will come to us. Most of us have been told from childhood that God is everywhere and so the most we can do is practice listening for that voice, trying to hear it in words and singing, in conversation, and in dreams.

We also know from story after story in the Bible that the voice of God comes in the way that will be easiest for us to hear if we only have the imagination to do so.

To a king in a land where dreams were studied for their messages, it came in a dream. To a middle-eastern couple who welcomed strangers, it came as a guest's voice. Many years later, the message would come to astronomers via a star.

God chooses the medium we are most likely to understand. But that is only half of it. We also have to be open to what we hear, whether the message is one of glad tidings or a message that we have sinned and need to do better.

Sometimes, the voice of God startles somebody else awake and gives us an opportunity to overhear a message that is important for us. Maybe we think the message does not apply to us, but the fact is, God tries to get our attention in any way he can.

No matter how good we are, we all need to know that we do not always get things right and, often, we need an example of obedience that will get us moving in the right direction. And God wants to give us the help and the chance we need to get back on the right path. Who better for God to use than a unexpected person who surprises us, someone we never imagined as the instrument of God's gentle correction?

Throughout the centuries that God has made his dwelling with the human race and intervened in human history, we have never lacked for signs of his presence or the still small voice that speaks in our hearts of love, compassion, justice, mercy, and forgiveness for all who hear it—and even for all who do not.

And there have surely been times when, ready or not, our sin catches us by surprise, and we come to know it in our sleep, rushing to make amends when we awake. Maybe that, too, was the voice of God that we heard in our restless dreams.

Read the story of Abimelech again and reflect on the following questions:

Reflect on the last two years of your life and name any places or times when you think God was particularly active—guiding, protecting, or giving you a kick in the pants? How did you know?

When you have become aware of sinful behavior that you did not recognize at the time, what has been your reaction? How have you handled it? Did you thank God for that awareness and attempt to make amends?

Have you ever dismissed someone's words or example because you did not want them to be right or important to you?

Do you make a regular habit of inviting God both to comfort you and to challenge you?

Where is the voice of God loudest for you?

The Prayer of
THE KING WHO DREAMED ABOUT AN UNKNOWN GOD

You, Whose name I do not know,
    Why do you keep after me?
You call out my name is my sleep
    until sleep is impossible and I am left with your words
    and the revelation of your glory.
I have tried to be a good person
I have earnestly sought to do what is right
    and I have not always been successful.
Why do you come to me, naming my sin?
Unless you come not to condemn, but to free me,
    not to destroy, but to raise me up,
and to make me want your raising up.
I do not know yet if that is what I want
    but come around again some night
    and we will talk some more.
Amen.

THE KING WHO PRAYED FOR WISDOM

At Gibeon the LORD appeared to Solomon in a dream by night; and God said, "Ask what I should give you." And Solomon said, "You have shown great and steadfast love to your servant my father David, because he walked before you in faithfulness, in righteousness, and in uprightness of heart toward you; and you have kept for him this great and steadfast love, and have given him a son to sit on his throne today. And now, O LORD my God, you have made your servant king in place of my father David, although I am only a little child; I do not know how to go out or come in. And your servant is in the midst of the people whom you have chosen, a great people, so numerous they cannot be numbered or counted. Give your servant an understanding mind to govern your people, able to discern between good and evil; for who can govern this your great people?"

It pleased the LORD that Solomon had asked this. God said to him, "Because you have asked this, and have not asked for yourself long life or riches, or for the life of your enemies, but have asked for yourself understanding to discern what is right, I now do according to your word. Indeed I give you a wise and discerning mind; no one like you has been before you and no one like you shall arise after you. I give you also what you have not asked, both riches and honor all your life; no other king shall compare with you. If you will walk in my ways, keeping my statutes and my commandments, as your father David walked, then I will lengthen your life."

Then Solomon awoke; it had been a dream. He came to Jerusalem where he stood before the ark of the covenant of the LORD. He offered up burnt offerings and offerings of well-being, and provided a feast for all his servants.

I KINGS 3:5–15

||||||||||||||||||||||||||||||||

The Backstory

Solomon is the son of King David and his wife, Bathsheba. While his story takes up the first eleven chapters of the first book of Kings, he is probably best known for three things: his wisdom, his wealth, and his construction of the first temple in Jerusalem.

His whole story reveals a somewhat more complex character—a good man who fails on occasion to do everything that is right. In other words, he is much like us.

He comes to the throne largely through the efforts of his mother, who wants to see her favorite succeed David. In this she is like Rebecca in Genesis, who plots to have Jacob receive Isaac's blessing, which rightfully belonged to Esau, the eldest son.

Among the more famous stories about Solomon are the ones involving the two women who claimed to be the mother of the same child, and the story about the visit of the queen of Sheba.

The first was meant to illustrate the wisdom for which Solomon prayed. He uncovers the real mother with his suggestion that the child be divided in two. The real mother willingly gives up her claim so that the child might live. That story comes immediately after Solomon's prayer above, in I Kings 3:15.

Following that, through various means, the biblical text brings out the wisdom of Solomon which impresses and draws rulers from around the world. Very little mention is made of the wealth he also accumulated.

But the story of the queen of Sheba, who comes to test Solomon's wisdom (I Kings 10:1–13), both emphasizes Solomon's wisdom and his great wealth, to which the queen adds enormous amounts. Following her visit, Solomon seems to go on a personal spending spree, creating thrones of ivory, cups of pure gold, and much more.

In I Kings 10:23, the verse reads: "Thus King Solomon excelled [surpassed] all the kings of the earth in riches and in wisdom." For the first time the riches are mentioned first. After that, the text records that Solomon began to worship other gods. Even so, the Lord did not forsake him. But the kingdom over which Solomon ruled was divided in two after his death as punishment for his unfaithfulness.

In the Christian Bible, the books of Kings are part of the historical books that impart the history of Israel. For Jews, though, the books of Kings are part of the prophetic books (along with Joshua, Judges, and the books of Samuel, who are called the *former prophets)* that use the stories of history to call their listeners to faithfulness to the commands of God.

⁞⁞⁞⁞⁞⁞⁞⁞⁞⁞⁞⁞⁞⁞⁞⁞⁞⁞⁞⁞⁞⁞⁞⁞⁞
What Does This Story Tell Us?

In the Hebrew Scriptures, God's habit of appearing in dreams to have important conversations may seem odd. But, during sleep we are vulnerable, open, and able to hear the suggestions of the unconscious inner self or the divine One who is outside us.

God waits precisely for such moments in our lives when we can name what we most desire, speak what is in our minds and hearts, and lay both our burdens and our joys into God's hands. And sometimes, God has to wait until we are asleep, because we are too distracted when awake.

One of the things we learn about God in this story is that God will often wait patiently for us to recognize his presence, no matter how long that takes, and then tell us: "Ask what I should give you."

In that moment we have two choices: we can turn inward to ourselves selfishly and ask for creature comforts and luxuries, or we can look outward at the face of Love and ask for whatever we need to serve God and to love one another well. In this passage, Solomon gives us an example of the latter.

In his prayer, Solomon demonstrates some of the characteristics needed to respond to one's vocation.

First, we have to recognize our gifts and our call as graces from God and accept our responsibility to do all for God's glory.

Second, we have to decide what is important to us and set our priorities.

And third, we have to acknowledge our limitations and our weaknesses and ask for what we need.

To pray for understanding is to admit that we don't always understand. To ask for discernment is to concede that sometimes the difference between good and evil is not always clear and that we may not always get it right. Solomon asks for both of these so that he might know what is right as he governs the people of Israel.

Everyone who leads—parents, presidents, pastors, teachers, ministers of all kinds—struggles with the temptations of power and the need to be in control.

Prayer is a way of saying that we are all in God's hands, and with that comes humility, a sense of service, and the understanding that we will surely make mistakes and occasionally fail altogether.

By the end of his life, Solomon reversed his priorities, placing wealth before wisdom. He forgot what was important and the humility that comes from service. That decision came with grave consequences for him and for his country. But he showed us the right way to begin our journeys, even in our dreams, so that we might find the grace to love God and those around us.

〃〃〃〃〃〃〃〃〃〃〃〃〃〃〃

Meditation for Groups or Individuals

Hundreds of years after Solomon lived and died, Jesus would tell his disciples that they could ask anything in his name and God would give it to them. When he got more specific and asked "What do you want me to do for you," James and John did not take a lot of time to set priorities.

Actually, they did not think much beyond themselves at all and asked for a place of honor in the time to come (Mark 10:35–45). The blind Bartimaeus, on the other hand, who had been intent on getting money, heard such a personal question, opened his heart and asked for his deepest desire: "My teacher, let me see again" (Mark 10:46–52). How do we set our priorities and acknowledge our weaknesses and need for God's grace?

It is clear that even after the example of Solomon, faithful people struggled when they were told to ask what God should give them. It is easy to ask for what we want, especially when it involves the immediate rewards of fame and good fortune.

When we get them we can say to the world, "See how much I am loved and admired." It is a great deal harder to ask for what we need when we recognize that our need also reveals our weakness and the place where we can be tempted most.

Such holes in our hearts and minds can be filled only by God. We need a large measure of humility to enter deeply into the heart, name our need, and then ask God for it—whether it is wisdom, courage, love, patience, humility itself, or the ability to see God rightly.

At least one time in his life, Solomon was able to do that, and God rewarded him with a discerning heart that drew people from all over the world. What if God is waiting right now to hear what we most need to live a life of faith in this world? What would we say?

Read the story again and reflect on the following questions:

Solomon asked for understanding and discernment of good from evil, both traits equated with wisdom. What would you ask God for if given the opportunity?

Sometimes, knowing what we really need in our hearts is easy and sometimes very difficult. If you weren't sure what you really needed to be a disciple, how would you go about finding out?

Where in your life have you been wisest? Where have you been most foolish? In what area would you like to gain wisdom?

Of all these questions and answers, which one(s) seems to stand out?
Spend some time in quiet reflection, asking God to reveal whatever
God needs to show you in your question and answer.

The Prayer of
THE KING WHO PRAYED FOR WISDOM

"Ask what you want," You say to me, Lord,
     But how do I know what I want
     when there are so many things to ask for?
I would love a return to my youth
     or the carefree joy of innocence.
I would like to have enough not to worry about
     what I wear or what I eat or how I get to where I am going.
"Search your heart," You say, "for what you need to
     to be my Child, my disciple, the best that
     I have called you to be.
Whatever you ask in my Son's name, I will give you."
Lord, let me understand your ways,
     and if I cannot understand them,
     let me cling to them as best I can.
Lord, give me a little wisdom
     to know when I am following your path and when I am not.
And when I am not, gently correct me
     and lead me to do your will.
Lord, give me your love
     which will guide and comfort me
And I shall have no need for anything else.
Amen.

Write your own prayer to God, asking for what you need right
now to do what God needs done.

SOME SUGGESTIONS FOR GROUP REFLECTION

The format for this book is designed for easy use for individuals who want to read, meditate, and pray on these stories. But each section can easily be adapted for a small group. For those who choose that option, you may find the following suggestions helpful.

Provide a copy of the passage, the questions for reflection, the prayer for each participant, (and meditation, if desired) and paper and pen for writing down thoughts.

The group leader should be prepared to provide the backstory or context for the passage and to facilitate any discussion about the teaching.

Welcome people to the session and invite participants to find a comfortable sitting posture. Open in prayer

If desired, the leader might pose an opening general question: "What does God have in common with mothers?" "When you hear the word 'lovers,' what do you think of?"

Have someone read the passage out loud slowly. Encourage people to simply listen and not read along. Afterward, give people a minute or two of silence to write down whatever they remember, what questions might surface, or anything about the passage.

Have someone read the passage again and take another minute for people to write down anything else they remember.

Invite participants to name the things that the passage brought up for them, including questions about the characters, words, or phrases that stuck out. Hang on to questions—they don't necessarily have to be answered at this time.

The leader can fill in some of the gaps with the backstory, talking a little about where the story comes in the larger context.

The leader can pose other questions: What does this story or this character tell us about God? A second might be, What do we learn about ourselves from this story? Are there points of similarity between you and the character? As discussion progresses, the leader can suggest some things by drawing from the section *What Does This Story Tell Us?*

Invite people into a comfortable position for the meditation. The leader can read the meditation aloud (and can take license with the wording) or participants can read the meditation for themselves and jot down answers to one or more of the questions posed at the end of the meditation. Allow a suitable amount of personal time for this.

Share aloud as a group as is appropriate or desired.

Close by reading the prayer together.